READERS' RAVES

Compliments from fans of Uncle John's Bathroom Reader.
(Aww shucks. We're blushing.)

"The *Bathroom Readers* rock. I read them everywhere!
Thank you so much for your endless supply of humor.
Keep 'em coming!"
—Cathy A., age 11

"My family and I absolutely love your books. I love to read
but hate getting into a heavy book at bedtime so I pick up
one of your books and read as much as I like before putting
it down to sleep. Keep up the good work! We love you!"
—Chrissy L.

"My son is 16 and has been reading the *BR* since he was
9. We have them all. Thanks for this great form of reading
pleasure."
—Glenda S.

"I LOVE the *Bathroom Readers for Kids Only.* I have
all three! My dad even reads them! He's a fully-grown
43-year-old kid, but we both love them! Cheers to Uncle
John, Porter the Wonder Dog, Elbow Room, and all of
you cool writers in the BRI! Go with the flow! (I always
wanted to say that. Heehee)"
—Ninon, age 11

"Hi!!!!!!!!! I absolutely LOVE your books!!!!!!!! I'm
absolutely OBSESSED. I now have a grand total of seven
Bathroom Readers and am working up to my eighth.
KEEP UP THE FABULOUS WOP""

"Thanks so much for the *Bathroom Readers*! My kids fight over them. (I like reading mine, too.) Thanks!"
—Marino Nardelli, 6th Grade Teacher

"Please, don't stop! I don't know what I would do without you. Uncle John, I pledge my undying love."
—Jeff A., age 9

"Thank you so much for your fantastic books! I regularly spout random trivia in school, and astound and amaze teachers and friends. Thanks for giving me more knowledge than any 12-year-old has a right to know."
—Hank J.

"I am writing this letter to express how much I have enjoyed your series. Watching TV bores me and these books do not show reruns. They keep me occupied for hours. When will another book be coming out?"
—Julie M., age 12

"You've addicted my family, my sister's family, and several friends…and the list grows!"
—Debby T.

"I absolutely love E-V-E-R-Y single one of your books! I ask for them on my birthday, on Christmas! I tell everyone all the fun facts I've learned from your books, who knew the dot on the "i" is called a "tittle"? Please continue publishing these books!!! They're great!"
—Derek B., age 11

"A bathroom without Uncle John is just a toilet."
—Chris L.

Uncle John's BOOK of FUN

by the
Bathroom Readers'
Institute

HA!

Bathroom Readers' Press
Ashland, Oregon

UNCLE JOHN'S
BOOK OF FUN
BATHROOM READER®
FOR KIDS ONLY

For information, write:
Bathroom Readers' Institute
P.O. Box 1117, Ashland, OR 97520
www.bathroomreader.com

Cover and book design by Michael Brunsfeld,
San Rafael, CA (*Brunsfeldo@comcast.net*)

Uncle John's Book of Fun
Bathroom Reader For Kids Only
by The Bathroom Readers' Institute

ISBN: 1-59223-259-0
Library of Congress Control Number: 2004110249

Printed in the United States of America

First printing 2004

10 9 8 7 6 5 4 3 2

UNCLE JOHN SEZ...

What's the most important ingredient in writing our books? Laughter. We love to laugh and we know you do, too. So we wrote a book devoted to fun—fun stuff to do, fun facts to tell, and, most importantly, funny jokes. The most difficult part was just to stop laughing long enough to write everything down. But we did it, and here it is, our first *Uncle John's Book of Fun.*

Before you giggle so hard you wet your pants (please don't wet your pants), let me give a special thank you to our joke writers and collectors, Jahnna, Malcolm, and Maggie M., to our book designer, Michael B., to our typesetter/page designer extraordinaire, Jeff A., and to all the crazy staff at the Bathroom Readers' Institute. Ha-ha. And, as always,

Go with the Flow.

—Uncle John

THANK YOU!

Gordon Javna	Maggie McLaughlin	Alan Orso
Jahnna Beecham	Dash and Skye	John Gaffey
Malcolm Hillgartner	Caitlin and	JoAnn Padgett
Jeff Altemus	McKenzie	Annie McIntyre
Michael Brunsfeld	Julia Papps	Laura Blackfeather
Thom Little	Sharilyn Hovind	Mustard Press
Jay Newman	Paul Stanley	Mana Manzavi
Brian Boone	Rick Rebhun	Porter the
Angela Kern	Amy Briggs	Wonder Dog
Sydney Stanley	John Dollison	Thomas Crapper

Pop Quiz

What will reading the
Gross Jokes and
the **Gross Songs**
in this book make you do?
Unscramble these words to find out.

A. F R A B
B. U R H L
C. P E K U
C. LLA FO HET VEBOA

WARNING TO PARENTS!
Whatever you do, don't read
YOU'RE GROUNDED
because
that's where your
kids will find cool ways to
prank their friends.

KNOCK KNOCK JOKES

Knock-knock!
Who's there?
Cargo.
Cargo who?
Car go
beep-beep!

What do you get when you cross a Bloodhound with a Labrador?
A Blabador—it never stops barking.

Animal Jokes

What do you get when you cross a Pekingese with a Lhasa Apso?
A Peekasso—an artistic dog.

What do you get when you cross a Deerhound with a Terrier?
A Derriere—a dog that's true to the end!

What do you get when you cross a Great Pyrenees with a Dachshund?
A Pyredachs (paradox)—a puzzling breed.

What do you get when you cross a Collie with a Lhasa Apso?
A Collapso—a dog that folds up for easy transport!

What do you get when you cross a Pointer with a Setter?
A Poinsetter (poinsettia)—a traditional Christmas pet.

What do you get when you cross a Spitz with a Chow?
A Spitz-Chow—a dog that barfs a lot!

What do you get from a cow that jumps up and down?

A milkshake!

WHAT DO YOU CALL A RABBIT OWNED BY A BEETLE?

A BUG'S BUNNY.

What's striped and jumps?

A zebra with hiccups.

WHAT'S SPOTTED AND BOUNCY?

A LEOPARD ON A TRAMPOLINE!

What do you get when you cross a bear with a skunk?

Winnie the Pew!

Why did the robin go to the library?

To find bookworms!

A SILLY RIDDLE

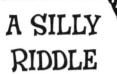

Two girls are walking down the street. They look alike, have the same mother and father, and were born at the same time. But they are not twins. What are they?

Triplets. (The other sister stayed home.)

Riddles & Brain Teasers

What did the baby banana say to the mama banana?

I don't peel good.

I give you a group of three:

One is sitting down and will never get up.

The second eats as much as is given to him, yet is always hungry.

The third goes away and never returns.

Stove, fire, smoke.

Why would a spider make a good outfielder?

He's good at catching Flies!

What do you call a hippie's wife?

Mississippi.

What begins with a T, ends with a T, and has T in it?

A teapot.

If a man carried my burden,

He would break his back.

I am not rich,

But I leave silver in my track.

A snail.

Jokes

Tee Hee *Ho Ho!* *Tee Hee...* *Yuk!*

PUNNY DEFINITIONS

Camelot—Where camels are parked.

Denial—A river in Egypt.

Igloo—An icicle built for two.

Polygon—A dead parrot.

chortle...

Violin—A very bad hotel.

Q: What do you call a squirrel's home?
A: A Nutcracker Suite.

Ha!

Schools—Mental institutions.

Busboy—A dish jockey.

Icicle—Stiff upper drip.

Dieting—Mind over platter.

Yuk!

Acorn—An oak in a nutshell.

Barber—The town cutup.

G—The end of everything.

Moon—A skylight.

HA! *Yuk!* *HA!* *HA!* *HO HO!*

TeeHee... *chortle...*

Recipes

FRUITY-PUTTY

This goopy stuff is not only colorful, it also smells great and you can eat it!

What You Need

- A stove
- 2 to 3 sheets wax paper
- 1 pot (2-qt.)
- 1 airtight plastic container

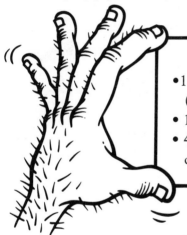

Ingredients

- 1 package Jell-O (any flavor)
- 1 cup salt
- 4 tablespoons cream of tartar
- 2 cups flour
- 2 cups boiling water
- 2 tablespoons vegetable oil

Preparation

Mix the dry ingredients in the pot. Add the boiling water (carefully!) and vegetable oil. Turn the heat to medium-high and stir the mixture until it forms into a ball. Place the ball on a sheet of wax paper to cool.

Experiment with different flavors and colors. Store your Fruity-Putty in the airtight container.

B-R-R-R-i-N-G

GREAT PRANK CALLS

Prankster: Hi, is Mr. Walls there?

Victim: No.

Prankster: Is Mrs. Walls there?

Victim: No.

Prankster: Are there *any* Walls there?

Victim: No.

Prankster: Well, if there's no Walls in your house, you'd better get out before the roof falls in!

Prankster: Hello, is Mr. Dean there?

Victim: No, sorry, you must have the wrong number.

Prankster: Can I leave a message?

Victim: No. You have the wrong number.

Prankster: Sorry. 'Bye.

Call back five minutes later, and repeat the first call. Call back five minutes after that and say: "Hello, this is Mr. Dean. Did I get any messages."

Disappearing Lions

Two lions were lying next to each other one evening. By the next morning, the two had completely disappeared, but they hadn't walked or run away. What happened?

Answers are on next page.

Brain Teasers

Rising Tide

The *Equinox* is a charter boat in Hawaii. It takes divers out to the reefs surrounding the islands. The divers use a rope ladder hung over the side of the boat to get in and out of the water. The ladder, which has five rungs that are eight inches apart, barely reaches the water. How many rungs will be under the water when the tide rises four feet?

Five Men in the Rain

Five men were going down a country road when it began to rain. Four of the men walked faster, but the fifth man made no effort to speed up. Yet, when they arrived at their destination together, the fifth man was dry and the other four were soaking wet. Why?

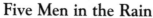

Solutions

ANSWERS FOR BRAIN TEASERS ON PREVIOUS PAGE.

Disappearing Lions
The lions were animal crackers.
They were eaten.

Rising Tide
No rungs will be underwater!
When the tide rises four feet,
the boat and its ladder
will also rise.

Five Men in the Rain
Four men were carrying a
coffin with the fifth man inside.

THAR SILLY SCIENCE
SHE BLOWS!

How to make your own volcano.

What You Need
- Modeling clay
- 1 tablespoon baking soda
- 2 to 3 drops red food coloring
- 2 to 3 drops liquid dishwashing soap
- 1/4 cup vinegar

Note: Things will get wet and messy wherever you do this experiment, so be sure to do it on a surface that can get wet. Set up the experiment on some old newspapers and be ready to clean up a mess!

Preparation: Use the clay to model your volcano. *Hint:* Using red clay around the rim makes it look like red-hot lava.

Scoop out a hole at the top of the volcano and stir in the baking soda, a few drops of red food coloring, and a few drops of liquid dishwashing soap. When you want your volcano to blow, pour the vinegar in the hole…and get out of the way!

21

MATH-MAGICAL

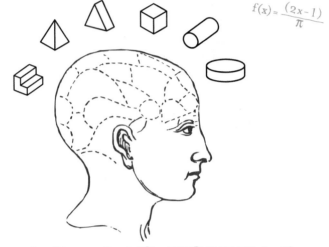

$$f(x) = \frac{(2x-1)}{\pi}$$

$$\frac{11}{16} - \frac{3}{8} < 1$$

AMAZE YOUR FRIENDS

You'll need a calculator to work this mind-bender.

• Have your friend think of a number between 1 and 100, and keep it a secret.

• Now, using your calculator, do the following steps:

> 1. Multiply your age by 2.
> 2. Add 5.
> 3. Multiply by 50.
> 4. Subtract 365.

• Next, keep the number from the last step on the calculator, hand the calculator to your friend, and tell them to:

> 1. Add their secret number.
> 2. Then add 115.

The first half of the resulting number is your age; the other part of the number is your friend's secret number!

A man was flying home from a business trip when the flight attendant handed out gourmet brownies and cookies. He wasn't hungry, so he decided to save them for later, and he put them in the cleanest thing he could find—an unused vomit bag.

After the plane landed, the man got up to leave and a flight attendant approached him. She asked, "Sir, would you like for me to dispose of that for you?"

"No thanks," he said. "I'm saving it for my kids."

Five guys were on a plane: a kid, a preacher, a doctor, the pilot, and a lawyer. The pilot came on the intercom and said, "Mayday! Mayday! We're going down, and there are only four parachutes on the plane. You decide who's staying, but I'm jumping now!"

The doctor said, "I've saved lives my whole life so I think that I should get one," and he jumped.

The lawyer said, "I'm the smartest man in the world. I've won hundreds of cases, so I'm jumping—bye!"

The preacher went up to the kid and said, "I've lived a long and happy life and I know I'm going to heaven, so you take the last parachute and go."

The kid said, "No, you can take this one. I can take the other one—the smartest man in the world just jumped out with my book bag!"

There was a woman with four husbands.
One was a millionaire, one was an
actor, one was a hairdresser,
and one was a limo driver.

One of the woman's friends asked her,
"Why do you need four husbands?"

The lady said, "One for the money,
two for the show, three to get
ready, and four to go!"

Riddles & Jokes

If you take two apples from three apples, how many do you have?

Two apples!

Which U.S. president's last name becomes a dance when "a" is added to the end of it?

Polk becomes Polka.

What should you take along on a trek in the desert?

A thirst-aid kit.

What do you get if you cross a galaxy and a toad?

Star warts.

Born at the same time as the world, destined to live as long as the world, yet never five weeks old. What am I?

The moon.

What has 50 heads and 50 tails?

Fifty pennies.

Where does a lamb go for a haircut?

To a baa-baa shop.

A man was telling his neighbor, "I just bought a new hearing aid. It cost me $4,000, but it's state of the art."

"Really?" asked the neighbor. "What kind is it?"

"Twelve-thirty."

There were three hunters: a Frenchman, an Englishman, and a stupid man. When the Frenchman caught a rabbit, the stupid man asked, "How did you catch it?"

The Frenchman replied, "I followed the tracks and caught the rabbit."

The next day, the Englishman caught a moose, and the stupid man asked, "How did you do that?"

The Englishman replied, "I followed the tracks and caught the moose."

Then the stupid man went out and came back empty-handed...but all beat up. The Frenchman and the Englishman asked, "What happened?"

The stupid man replied, "I followed the tracks and got hit by the train."

Les and Paul each have a collection of baseballs. Les said that if Paul would give him four of his baseballs, they would have an equal number; but if Les would give Paul four of his balls, Paul would have three times as many balls as Les. How many balls each do Les and Paul have?

The answer is on the next page.

Solution

Answer from previous page.

PLAY BALL!

Les has 12 balls; Paul has 20 balls. If Paul gives Les 4 balls, they would have an equal number (16 baseballs each). If Les gives Paul 4 balls, then Paul would have 24 and Les would have 8, so Paul would have 3 times as many baseballs as Les.

LIMERICKS

There was a young lady of Kent,
Whose nose was most awfully bent.
She followed her nose
One day, I suppose...
Because no one knows which
way she went.

If you find
for your verse
there's no call,

And you
can't afford
paper at all,

For the poet
true born,

However
forlorn,

There's always
the bathroom
wall.

I went with the duchess to tea.
Her manners were shocking
to see;
Her rumblings abdominal
Were simply phenomenal,
And everyone thought it was me!

Said the vet as he looked at my pet:
"That's the skinniest bear that I've met.
I'll soon alter that."
Now the bear's nice and fat.
The question is: Where is the vet?

A man stood before the Pearly Gates and St. Peter asked him, "Have you done anything in your life that would qualify you to enter heaven?"

"Well, I can think of one thing," the man offered. "Once, on a trip to the Black Hills, out in South Dakota, I came upon a gang of bikers who were threatening an old lady. I told them to leave her alone, but they wouldn't listen. So I went right up to the biggest, most heavily tattooed biker. I whacked him on the head, kicked his bike over, ripped out his nose ring and threw it on the ground, and told him 'Leave her alone now, or you'll answer to me!'"

St. Peter was impressed. "When did this happen?"

"Just a couple of minutes ago."

the Graffiti Page

Are female moths called myths?

SO WHAT IS THE SPEED OF DARK?

How do you know when you've run out of invisible ink?

Do vegetarians eat animal crackers?

GRAVITY— It's the law!

DO HEARSES GET TO USE THE CAR POOL LANE?

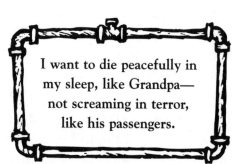

I want to die peacefully in my sleep, like Grandpa— not screaming in terror, like his passengers.

Would a fly without wings be called a walk?

"My one regret in life is that I'm not someone else."
—Woody Allen

Roses are red,
Violets are blue.
I copied your test,
And I failed, too.

Moses and Jesus were part of a threesome playing golf one day. Moses pulled up to the tee and drove a long shot. The ball landed in the fairway, but then rolled directly into a water trap. Quickly Moses raised his club, the water parted, and the ball rolled to the other side, safe and sound.

Next, Jesus strolled up to the tee and hit a nice long one directly toward the same water trap. It landed right in the center of the pond and hovered over the water. Jesus casually walked out on the pond and chipped the ball right up onto the green.

The third guy got up and whacked the ball over the fence and into oncoming traffic on a nearby street. It bounced off a truck and hit a nearby tree.

From there, it bounced onto the roof of a shack close by and rolled down into the gutter, down the drainpipe, out onto the fairway, and straight toward the pond. On the way to the pond, the ball hit a little stone and bounced out over the water and onto a lily pad, where it rested quietly.

Suddenly, a very large bullfrog jumped up onto the lily pad and snatched the ball into his mouth. Just then, an eagle swooped down and grabbed the frog and flew away. As they passed over the green, the frog dropped the ball, which bounced right into the hole for a beautiful hole-in-one.

Moses turned to Jesus and said,
"I hate playing with your dad."

A TRUE STORY

A man named Stephen R. King was arrested in California when he tried to hold up a bank. The only problem: King had no weapon—he used his thumb and forefinger to make it look like he had a gun in his pocket. It almost worked, too. Until he forgot...and pulled the "gun" out of his pocket.

A customer walks into a sporting goods store and asks the salesman, "Do you have any cockroaches?"

"Yeah, we sell 'em to fishermen."

"Great! I'd like 20,000 of them."

"Twenty thousand cockroaches! You've got to be kidding! Why do you need that many?"

"I'm moving tomorrow," the customer explains, "and my lease says I must leave my apartment in the same condition I found it in."

Jokes

Ho Ho!

Tee Hee...

Tee Hee...

Yuk!

Ho Ho!

Tee Hee...

A mushroom goes to a party, where he walks up to a girl and asks her to dance.

"I'm not dancing with you," she says.

"Aw, come on," the mushroom says. "Why not? I'm a fungi."

Yuk!

Yuk!

HA!

Tee Hee...

Tee Hee...

Yuk!

Tee Hee...

chortle...

Ho Ho!

Yuk!

chortle...

chortle...

Ho Ho!

HA!

YUK!

Ha!

Malcolm's sister had baby twins, a boy and a girl, but she couldn't decide what to name them.

When the doctor visited her, she said, "Doctor, I still haven't named my children."

"Don't worry," he replied. "Your brother named them."

"What are their names?"

"Denise and Denephew"

YUK!

HA!

Yuk!

HA!

Ho Ho!

HO HO!

HA!

Tee Hee...

chortle...

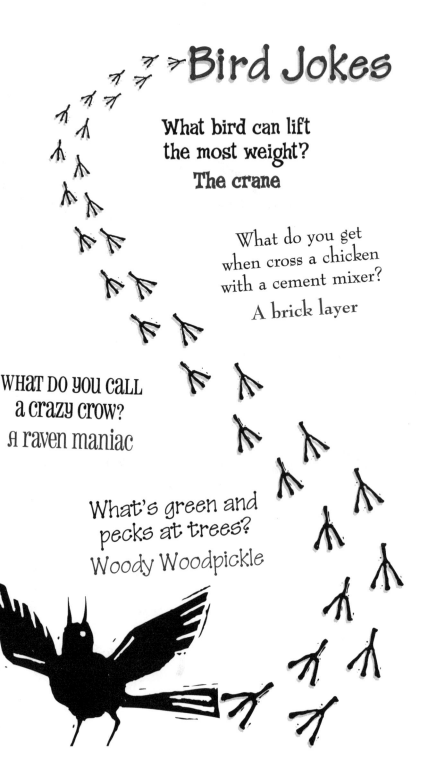

Bird Jokes

What bird can lift
the most weight?
The crane

What do you get
when cross a chicken
with a cement mixer?
A brick layer

WHAT DO YOU CALL
a crazy crow?
A raven maniac

What's green and
pecks at trees?
Woody Woodpickle

Doctor! Doctor! I keep hearing a ringing sound!

Try answering the phone.

WHAT KIND OF FILMS DO GEESE LIKE TO WATCH?

DUCK-UMENTARIES

What word is always pronounced wrong?

"Wrong."

Jokes

Jokes

How many magicians does it take to change a lightbulb?

It depends on what you want to change it into.

How many mystery writers does it take to change a lightbulb?

Two. One to screw it almost all the way in, and the other to give it a surprising twist at the end.

Jokes

EXTREME SPOONS

This is a fun card game that should be played outside. What makes this game "extreme" is the speed at which you play and the location of the spoons. Object of the game: Collect four cards of one kind and grab a spoon.

What You Need

One deck of cards, three or more players, and spoons (one fewer than the number of players).

How to Play

1. Place the spoons in a row within running distance from the circle of the game. If you're in public, be sure you have a clear path between you and the spoons; don't run over innocent bystanders.

2. Each player gets four cards and the dealer keeps the deck. Remember: The faster the game is played, the more fun it is.

3. The dealer picks a card from the deck and then discards one card from his hand, sliding it face down to the player to his left. That player takes it, then passes one card from his hand to the player on *his* left.

4. Each player in turn does the same, as fast as possible. Each person should have four cards in their hand at all times. The player to the right of the dealer places discarded cards in a pile to his left, to be used by the dealer when the original deck is used up.

5. Play continues until one player has four of a kind, at which time he runs as fast as he can to grab a spoon. As soon as the first person goes for a spoon, everyone else does, too. No cheating! The player who initiated the spoon run *must* have four of a kind.

6. The player left without a spoon has lost the round.

Rookie baseball player: How do you hold a bat?

Old-timer: By its wings.

WHAT DO FISH SAY WHEN THEY HIT A CONCRETE WALL?

"DAM!"

What do sheep do on sunny days?

Have a baa-baa-cue.

HOW DO YOU CATCH A UNIQUE RABBIT?

UNIQUE UP ON IT.

HOW DO YOU CATCH A TAME RABBIT?

TAME WAY— UNIQUE UP ON IT.

If the dictionary goes from A to Z, what goes from Z to A?

A zebra.

WHY DID THE PONY COUGH?

He was a LITTLE HORSE.

What's little and quick and has 32 wheels?

A spider on roller skates!

Little Johnny was in the garden filling in a hole when his neighbor peered over the fence. "What are you up to there, Johnny?" the neighbor asked.

"Well, my goldfish died," replied Johnny tearfully, without looking up, "and I've just buried him."

The neighbor saw the big mound of dirt and remarked, "That's an awfully big hole for a goldfish." Johnny patted down the last heap of dirt and replied, "That's because he's inside your cat!"

Silly Songs & Rhymes

Speedy Sam,
while exploring
a cave,

Had what I
call a very
close shave.

He stepped
on a bear,

That had
dozed off
in there.

I'm glad he
was faster
than brave.

GOD BLESS MY UNDERWEAR
(Sung to the tune of "God Bless America")

God bless my underwear,
My only pair!
Stand beside them,
And guide them,
So they don't get a rip or a tear.
From the washer, to the dryer,
From the dresser, back to me.
God bless my underwear,
My only pair!

BE KIND TO YOUR
WEB-FOOTED FRIENDS

(Sung to the tune of "Three Cheers
for the Red, White, and Blue")
Be kind to your web-footed friends,
For a duck may be somebody's
       mother.
Be kind to the birds in the swamp,
When the weather's cold and damp.
Well, you may think
      that this is the end...
Well, it is.

SAY IT, DON'T SPRAY IT

A tongue twister.

A tree toad loved a she-toad
That lived up in a tree.
She was a three-toed tree toad
But a two-toed toad was he.
The two-toed toad tried to win
The she-toad's friendly nod,
For the two-toed toad loved the ground
On which the three-toed tree toad trod.
But no matter how the two-toed tree toad tried,
He could not please her whim.
In her three-toed power,
The three-toed she-toad vetoed him.

Jokes

Ho Ho!

Tee Hee...

Tee Hee...

Yuk!

What did the zero say to the eight?

"Nice belt!"

WHAT DO YOU CALL A PERSON WHO CRUNCHES THEIR CORN FLAKES?

A CEREAL KILLER.

Ho Ho!

Tee Hee...

Yuk!

Ho Ho!

Tee Hee...

Yuk!

Yuk!

HA!

Tee Hee...

chortle...

What do Eskimos get from sitting on the ice too long?

Polaroids.

Tee Hee...

chortle...

Ho Ho!
Yuk!

YUK!
HA!

chortle...

Ho Ho!

HA

YUK!

Ha!

WHAT DO YOU CALL FOUR BULLFIGHTERS in QUICKSAND? QUATRO SINKO.

"May I take your order?" the waiter asked.

"Yes. How do you prepare your chickens?"

"Nothing special, sir," he replied. "We just tell them straight out that they're going to die."

Yuk!
HA!

Ho Ho!

HO HO!

HA!

Tee Hee...

chortle...

46

Logic Puzzle

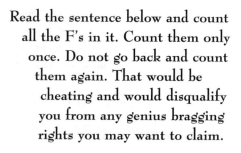

GOT BRAINS?
PROVE IT!

*There are no tricks to this intelligence test. But
be forewarned! It's not as easy as it looks.*

Read the sentence below and count
all the F's in it. Count them only
once. Do not go back and count
them again. That would be
cheating and would disqualify
you from any genius bragging
rights you may want to claim.

**FINISHED FILES ARE
THE RESULT OF YEARS
OF SCIENTIFIC STUDY
COMBINED WITH THE
EXPERIENCE OF YEARS.**

See your score on the next page.

Solution

GOT BRAINS?

There are 6 F's in the sentence.

If you found 3—you're about average.

If you spotted 4—hey, you're above average.

If you got 5—you're exceptional.

If you found all 6—you're a genius!

Most of us overlook the F's in the word "OF." That's because the human brain tends to see them as V's, not F's.

Monster Jokes

What should you say when you meet a ghost?

"How do you boo?"

WHAT DO monsters make with cars?

Traffic jam.

WHAT DO YOU CALL A VAMPIRE THAT LIVES IN THE KITCHEN?

COUNT SPATULA

What do little ghosts drink? Evaporated milk.

A little boy was playing by a pond when he saw a Port-A-Potty. Just for fun, he tipped it over into the pond, then he ran home. At dinner, his father told the story of how George Washington chopped down the cherry tree and told the truth to his father. Feeling guilty, the little boy 'fessed up and told his dad what he'd done at the pond.

Suddenly the boy's father yanked him out of his chair and started spanking him.

"Wait, Dad!" the boy cried, "I told the truth just like George Washington did when he chopped down the cherry tree! His dad didn't spank him."

"Yeah, but George's dad wasn't in the tree when he chopped it down!"

FUNNY ANSWERING MACHINE MESSAGES

A bubble in the space-time continuum has connected your line to a channeler in the 23rd century. Any message you leave will be broadcast into the future.

BEEP

You have reached the number you have dialed. Please leave a tone after the message.

Hi, i'm not home right now but my answering machine is, so talk to it instead.

Twinkle, twinkle, little star,
Bet you're wondering where we are.
Right now we can't get to the phone,
But we'll call back when we get home.
And if you make your message rhyme,
We'll call you back in half the time.

GAMES

MUMMY WRAP

Another action-packed party game.

What You Need
- Lots of rolls of toilet paper
- Large garbage bag (for clean-up)

How to Play

1. This game is best when there are lots of players. Divide into teams of four or more—one kid is the mummy, the others are the wrappers.

2. Give each wrapper at least one roll of toilet paper. The mummy stands in the center of his team.

3. On "GO!" each team races to wrap their mummy first. It's trickier than you think: The faster you try to wrap the mummy, the more likely the toilet paper will tear, which inevitably leads to...starting over.

DOG JOKES

What did the dog say when she dropped her ice cream?

"Doggone it!"

What do you get when you cross a Pit Bull with a Collie?

A dog that bites your leg, then goes for help.

Why shouldn't you loan books to a dog?

He'll make them dog-eared!

An elephant and a crocodile are swimming in the Congo River, when the elephant spots a turtle sunning himself on a rock. The elephant walks over to the turtle, picks him up in his trunk, and hurls him far into the jungle.

"What did you do that for?" asks the crocodile.

"That turtle was the one that bit me almost fifty years ago," the elephant replies.

"And you remembered him after all these years? Boy, you sure do have a good memory."

"Yep," says the elephant. "I have turtle recall."

ELEPHANT JOKES

Why did the little boy take two elephants into the pool with him?

He needed swimming trunks.

What do you get if you cross an elephant and a kangaroo?

Big holes all over Australia!

WHAT DID THE CAT SAY TO THE ELEPHANT?
MEOW.

How do you get an elephant out of the theater?

You can't. It's in his blood.

Why do elephants paint their toenails red?

So they can hide in the strawberry patch.

But there aren't any elephants in the strawberry patch!

See? Their camouflage is working.

Graffiti

Yo' Mamma is so fat, I had to take a train and two buses just to get on her good side.

Time is what keeps everything from happening at once.

How many of you believe in telekinesis? Raise my hand.

If you can't convince them, confuse them.

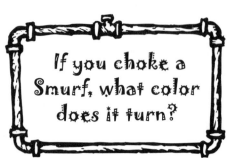

If you choke a Smurf, what color does it turn?

Weather forecast for tonight: dark.

I feel like I am diagonally parked in a parallel universe.

WHEN YOU DON'T KNOW WHAT TO DO, DO IT NEATLY.

Christy: We can't go swimming right now. We just ate, and Mom said we shouldn't swim on a full stomach.

Laura: Okay, we'll swim on our backs.

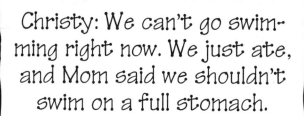

What did the judge say when the skunk walked into the courtroom?

"Odor in the court!"

WHAT DO YOU GET FROM A PAMPERED COW?

SPOILED MILK.

RiDDLes
& BrAin TeAsers

Joan is an only child. "I am going to a party," she said. "It's my mother's husband's daughter's birthday party." Whose party was it?

It was Joan's party.

What gets bigger as you take more out of it?

A hole.

A certain five-letter word becomes shorter when you add two letters to it. What is the word?

Short(er).

WHAT UNUSUAL WORD HAS THREE U'S IN IT?

Unusual.

George's mother had three children: one named April, one named May, and one named...what?

George.

WHAT STARTS WITH 'E' AND ENDS WITH 'E' AND CONTAINS ONLY ONE LETTER?

AN ENVELOPE.

A snail is out for a walk when four turtles mug him. After recovering his wits, he goes to make a police report. "Can you describe the turtles?" asks the officer.

"Not well, it all happened so fast," replies the snail.

You are traveling north on an electric train. The wind is headed south. You make two left turns. If the wind speed is faster than the train, what direction is the smoke from the train blowing?

An electric train doesn't blow smoke.

I happen once in every minute. Twice in every moment. I never happened at all in a thousand years. What am I?

The letter M

If you had one match and entered a room in which there were a kerosene lamp, an oil burner, and a wood-burning stove, which would you light first?

The match.

59

Classic Riddles

Two words—my
answer is only
two words.
To keep me,
You must give
me.

Your word.

All about, but
cannot be seen.
Can be captured,
cannot be held.
No throat, but
can be heard.

The wind.

Gentle enough to
soothe the skin,
Light enough to
caress the sky,
Hard enough to
crack rocks.
Who am I?

Water.

My life can be
measured in hours;
I serve by being
devoured.
Thin, I am quick,
Fat, I am slow.
Wind is my greatest
foe.

A candle.

MAGIC

THE PENDULUM OF TRUTH

*This pendulum always answers YES or NO,
even when you're not the one swinging it!*

What You Need

1 pendulum (basically, any
weight suspended from
a string. You can use
a heavy bead, a
fishing weight,
or a washer).

The Trick

Hold the pendulum
yourself, or have someone
else hold it. Whoever holds the pendulum must ask a question that can be answered "Yes" or "No." Without them doing
anything, the pendulum will start to swing—a straight line
for Yes; a circle for No. Even if the person holding the
pendulum tries to keep it still, it will always
swing to answer every question.

How It Works

No one can fully explain why this trick
works. Some say the subconscious effect of
the pendulum holder's thoughts influence
the way the pendulum swings...
or maybe it's just magic.

Limericks

There was a young man of Calcutta,

Who had a most terrible stutta,

He said: "Pass the h...h...am,

And the j...j... j...jam,

And the b... b... b... b... b... b... butta."

The fabulous Wizard of Oz
Retired from business becoz,

What with up-to-date science,

To most of his clients,

He wasn't the Wiz he once woz.

A monkey exclaimed with great glee:

"Oh the things in this zoo that I see!

Like the curious features

Of all those strange creatures

That come and throw peanuts at me!"

SAY IT, DON'T SPRAY IT

A tantalizing tumble of tongue twisters for the nimble of tongue.

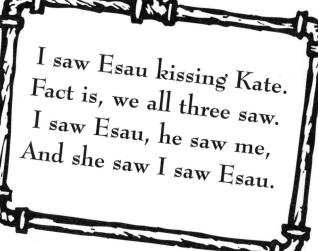

I saw Esau kissing Kate.
Fact is, we all three saw.
I saw Esau, he saw me,
And she saw I saw Esau.

Go, My Son

"Go, my son, and shut the shutter."
This I heard a mother mutter.
"Shutter's shut," the boy did mutter,
"I can't shut'er any shutter."

Recipes

RATTLESNAKE EGGS

Want to really scare someone? This is a good trick to play on a person you know is afraid of snakes.

What You Need

- 1 wire coat hanger
- 1 new rubber band
- 1 big button
- 1 size-10 envelope (4-1/8 x 9-1/2)
- 1 pair of pliers or wire cutters

Preparation:

Cut the rubber band and thread it through the button.
Use the wire cutters to snip off about 6 inches of coat hanger and shape it into a **⊏** . Tie the rubber band onto the ends of the coat hanger. Wind the button up fairly tightly. Load the device into the envelope and seal it (make sure the rubber band doesn't unwind). Write on the outside of the envelope: WARNING—Rattlesnake Eggs. KEEP REFRIGERATED! When the curious victim opens the envelope, the button will spin, making a rattling sound!

Jokes

Tee Hee...

Ho Ho!

Ho Ho!

Tee Hee...

A teacher asked a student, "Harry, can you form a sentence using the words defeat, deduct, defense, and detail?"

Harry replied, "Defeat of deduct jumped over defense before detail."

Yuk!

Ho Ho!

Tee Hee...

Yuk!

Tee Hee...

chortle...

HA!

Tee Hee...

chortle...

chortle...

Yuk!

HA!

Ho Ho!

HO HO!

A moron was in a canoe trying to paddle it through a field. Another moron walks up to the edge of the field and yells, "Hey, what are you doing?"

The first moron says, "I'm trying to paddle through the water, but it doesn't seem to be working."

The second moron says, "If I knew how to swim, I'd come out there and help!"

Ho Ho!

Yuk!

YUK!

HA!

Ho Ho!

HA!

YUK!

Ha!

HA!

Tee Hee...

chortle...

READ 'em and LAUGH!

Silly book titles we'd like to see.

Late Again
by Misty Buss

Where Is Everybody?
by I. Malone

Pain and Sorrow
by Anne Guish

A Call for Assistance
by Linda Hand

The Arctic Ocean
by I. C. Waters

The Big Bang
by Dina Mite

Sunday Service
by Neil Downe

The Hurricane
by Rufus Blownoff

Collecting Litter
by Phil D. Basket

Will He Win?
by Betty Wont

Kidnapped!
by Caesar Quick

Crossing Roads Safely
by Luke Bothways

Under the Bleachers
by Seymore Butts

The Haunted House
by Hugo Furst

The Yellow River
by I. P. Freely

The Chocolate Bar
by Ken I. Havesum

The Best Day Ever
by Trudy Light

Baker's Men
by Pat E. Cake

A History of Valentines
by Bea Mine

Grade School Is Easy
by Ella Mann Tree

FLOWER POWER

*Did you know that you can make flowers
turn different colors? Here's how.*

What You Need

- White flowers
- Food coloring
- 1/2 cup water
- Vase

Preparation

Put any white flower—like carnations,
roses, or daisies—in a vase with the water.
Put at least 10 drops of food coloring in the
water. Leave the flowers in the colored
water overnight. When you check your flowers in the morning, you'll find that the
petals have changed color. The longer you
leave the flowers in the colored water, the
more color you'll see in the petals.

How It Works

The food coloring travels up through the
stem by a process called *capillary action* and
seeps into the petals. Take a closer look at
the petals, and you can see the path the
food coloring traveled.

Jokes

What do hippies do?
Hold up your leggies.

Why is it hard to play cards in the jungle?
There are too many cheetahs.

What sport do flies hate the most?
Squash.

Jokes

Jokes

What did the Pacific Ocean say to the Atlantic Ocean?

Nothing. It just waved.

HOW DO ANTS KEEP WARM IN THE WINTER?
ANTI-FREEZE.

Jokes

Deep within a forest a little turtle began to climb a tree. After hours and hours of effort he reached the top, jumped into the air waving his front legs, and crashed to the ground.

After recovering, the little turtle slowly climbed the tree again, jumped, and fell to the ground. Banged up and bruised, the tough little turtle tried again and again while a couple of birds sitting on a branch watched his sad efforts.

Finally, the female bird turned to her mate. "Dear," she chirped, "I think it's time to tell him he's adopted."

 Silly Science

THE JITTERBUG COIN

What You Need

- Empty 2-liter plastic soda bottle
- Quarter
- Glass of Water

Preparation

1. Place the empty bottle (make sure it's uncapped) in the freezer for 10 minutes.

2. Dip the coin in the glass of water.

3. Remove the bottle from the freezer and immediately place the wet coin on the top of the open bottle. The coin will start to jiggle and move!

How It Works

When the bottle is taken out of the freezer, the cold air inside it expands and tries to rush out of the bottle. This jet of air is what makes the coin do the jitterbug.

*Answers are
on next page.*

A MEASURE OF RAIN

TWO FARMERS WERE TALKING OVER THE FENCE WHEN IT STARTED TO RAIN. ONE FARMER GRUMBLED MISERABLY AND SAID, "IT'S NOT FAIR, YOUR FARM ALWAYS GETS MORE RAIN THAN MINE." HOW COULD HE BE RIGHT?

A Stringy Problem

Chelsea puts a piece of string on some food and then throws it away. Why would she do this?

Stuck Truck

The driver of an 18-wheeler semi truck misjudged the height of a bridge and managed to get the truck stuck under it. Traffic was backed up for hours while engineers contemplated possible solutions. But a kid saved the day with the most logical strategy for getting the truck unstuck.

What did he suggest?

Solutions

ANSWERS FOR BRAIN TEASERS ON PREVIOUS PAGE.

A MEASURE OF RAIN

ONE FARMER HAD MORE LAND THAN THE OTHER.

A Stringy Problem

Chelsea was flossing her teeth.

Stuck Truck

The kid suggested they let some air out of the tires.

LOOK SMART!

Impress your friends with these weird facts.

There is only one insect that can turn its head completely around—the praying mantis.

Even though he wasn't blind, Thomas Edison preferred to read with his fingertips—he liked Braille better.

The honeybee has to travel an average of 43,000 miles to collect enough nectar to make a pound of honey.

MATH-MAGICAL

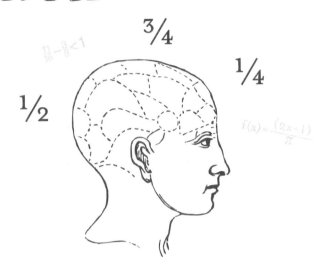

$3/4$

$1/4$

$1/2$

.*M*A*G*I*C 7*.

This trick is more impressive when you do it the old-fashioned way—with a pencil and paper.

1. Think of a number.

2. Subtract 2.

3. Multiply the result by 3.

4. Add 12.

5. Divide the result by 3.

6. Add 5.

7. Subtract the number you first thought of.

The answer is always 7.

DID YOU KNOW?

The largest recorded snowflake measured eight inches across—that's as big as a dinner plate!

The lungfish can live out of water for as long as four years.

SOME SPECIES OF FROGS CAN BE FROZEN SOLID, THEN THAWED...AND STILL BE ALIVE.

A hummingbird weighs less than a penny!

Foxes really are clever. To make their favorite meals come out of hiding, they sometimes nip the legs of cattle to make them stomp the ground. When the cattle stomp, mice and other rodents are frightened out of their burrows, and the sly foxes begin hunting.

IF YOU WERE BORN ON...

Hey, we've got your number. Find the day of your birth below and discover what numerology has to say about you.

The 1st Day of the Month: You are strong-willed and self-reliant. You know what you want and usually get it. Friends say you think too much, but you always do what you think is right.

The 2nd Day of the Month: Your strong desire for peace and harmony makes you very sensitive and highly aware of your environment. You are a good friend.

The 3rd Day of the Month: You are happy-go-lucky and love to have fun. To you, life is a party. You are generous, forgiving, sympathetic, and a great storyteller.

The 4th Day of the Month: You are responsible, practical, and reliable. You like to keep busy and take pride in your work. You love it when a plan comes together.

The 5th Day of the Month: You are incredibly curious. You love adventure and challenge. You are irresistibly charming (you knew that) and make friends easily.

The 6th Day of the Month: You are creative and artistic. Being a loyal and devoted person, family, friends, and community are important to you.

The 7th Day of the Month: You are a serious person, very intuitive, and have your own way of doing things. You definitely need your quiet time to meditate and relax.

The 8th Day of the Month: People look to you for leadership. You set your goals and then work tirelessly to achieve them. The truth is, you love to solve problems.

The 9th Day of the Month: You have a passionate need to make the world a better place. You seek wisdom rather than mere knowledge. You make friends easily.

The 10th Day of the Month: You are a self-confident leader. You are self-motivated and independent. You prefer to see the big picture and leave the details to others.

The 11th Day of the Month: You are a dreamer and an idealist. You know how to inspire people. You are very sensitive and intuitive. You are definitely creative.

The 12th Day of the Month: You are energetic, friendly, sensitive, imaginative, and naturally talkative. It's easy for you to express yourself—even in front of the class!

The 13th Day of the Month: You are a serious, honest, hardworking individual. You are aware of details, even to the point of being a perfectionist.

The 14th Day of the Month: You love to travel, meet new people, and face new challenges. You are talented, imaginative, versatile, and lucky in everything you do.

The 15th Day of the Month: You love people and are

concerned, generous, and tolerant. Things seem to always work out for you—especially when it comes to money.

The 16th Day of the Month: You are introspective, thoughtful, and fiercely independent. Even so, family is very important. Above all else, you are a unique individual.

The 17th Day of the Month: You are a money magnet! You are ambitious and succeed at everything you put your mind to. People naturally look to you for leadership.

The 18th Day of the Month: You are at your best when doing good deeds for others. Creative, compassionate, and generous, you know that the true gift is in the giving.

The 19th Day of the Month: You have a strong sense of confidence and purpose. You'd rather learn through experience than take advice or direction from someone else.

The 20th Day of the Month: You are sensitive and care a great deal about the feelings of others. You make friends quickly, but you can be nervous in large groups.

The 21st Day of the Month: You are an optimist, a big dreamer, and a people magnet. It's easy for you to communicate—which often helps make your dreams come true.

The 22nd Day of the Month: You want to make the world a better place. You are not afraid to take on big projects—as long as someone else takes care of the details.

The 23rd Day of the Month: You are charming, curious, and adventurous. You hate to be boxed in but know how to make the best of any situation.

The 24th Day of the Month: You have an artist's heart. You love all things beautiful. Your friends trust you and probably look to you as a counselor and a mediator.

The 25th Day of the Month: You are a private person—shy about showing your feelings. You have a mind for detail: science and other complex subjects interest you.

The 26th Day of the Month: You are ambitious, dedicated, and energetic. You have the ability to see the big picture and still attend to the fine details that bore others.

The 27th Day of the Month: You have the spirit of a humanitarian. You are at your best when helping others but still need your alone time to meditate and rejuvenate.

The 28th Day of the Month: You're a born leader with a will to succeed. You have self-confidence and determination. You find creative solutions to life's challenges.

The 29th Day of the Month: You are interested in spiritual matters and have good insight into the world around you. You will have a positive impact on many people.

The 30th Day of the Month: You are dramatic, imaginative and have a talent for words. Self-expression is critical for your happiness. Many people enjoy your company.

The 31st Day of the Month: You are a practical person, at your best when organizing a long-term project. Loving and loyal, you enjoy travel—but not alone!

EwW...GroSS

THE DEAD FINGER TRICK

This one's not for the faint of heart.

What You Need

- 1 small empty box
- Scissors
- Baby powder or white flour
- Red nail polish or ketchup
- A few cotton balls

Preparation: Cut a hole in the bottom of the box. Pack it with cotton balls. Smudge the cotton balls with ketchup or red nail polish. Rub the baby powder or flour on your finger to make it look dead white. Smear a bit of the ketchup or nail polish on your finger. Stick your "dead finger" up through the hole in the box, make sure to rest it on the bloody-looking cotton balls. Put the top on the box.

The Prank: Gather your friends or family members in a circle around you. Tell them you found something really horrible and disgusting… then slowly open the box.

Gross Jokes

Q: Did you hear the joke about the fart?

A: You don't want to, it stinks!

Teacher: I lost another pupil.

Principal: How did that happen?

Teacher: My glass eye flew out the window while I was driving.

At church one Sunday, a little boy said, "Mommy, I have to pee." The mother said, "It's not nice to say the word 'pee' in church. From now on, when you have to pee, just tell me that you have to 'whisper.'"

The following Sunday, the little boy went to church with his father and during the service he said, "Daddy, I have to whisper."

His dad looked at him and said, "Okay, why don't you just whisper in my ear?"

Q: Did you hear about the giant with diarrhea?

A: You didn't? It's all over town!

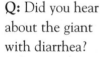

Q: What's the difference between roast beef and pea soup?

A: Anyone can roast beef.

Gross Songs

Mama's Soup Surprise

(sung to tune of
"Supercalifragilisticexpialidocious")

Oh, chicken lips and lizard hips
and alligator eyes,

Monkey legs and buzzard eggs
and salamander thighs,

Rabbit ears and camel rears
and tasty toenail pies,

Stir them all together and
it's Mama's soup surprise!

My Body Needs Calamine Lotion

(to the tune of "My Bonnie
Lies over the Ocean")

My body needs calamine lotion;

My body's as sore as can be,

The flowers I picked for my mother

Turned out to be poison ivy.

Artsy-Fartsy

O n Grandma's 100th birth- day, the family wheeled her onto the lawn in her wheelchair for a picnic. When she slowly started to lean to the right, her daughter stuffed a pillow on her right side to prop her up.

A few minutes later, she started leaning to her left. Another family member caught her and straightened her up, stuffing a pillow on her left side. Soon she started tilting forward. This time her son caught her and tied a pillow around her waist.

A few minutes later, her nephew arrived. He said, "Hey, Grandma! How's life treating you?"

Grandma, who could no longer speak, took out her notepad and wrote, "Terrible. They won't let me fart."

Insults

YO' MAMA IS SO FAT...

- ...her cereal bowl came with a lifeguard.

- ...her driver's license says, "Picture continued on other side."

- ...when she dances she makes the band skip.

- ...she sat on a camel and flattened its hump!

- ...she's got smaller fat women orbiting around her.

- ...she has to put her belt on with a boomerang.

- ...when she turns around, people throw her a welcome-back party.

- ...all the restaurants in town have signs that say "Maximum Occupancy: 240 patrons OR yo' mama."

- ...when she goes to the ocean the whales start singing "We Are Family."

HOW INSULTING!

Yo' daddy is so old, he owes Moses $1.50.

Yo' mama's so stupid, you have to dig for her IQ!

Yo' sister is so ugly, when she was little her mother used to tie a pork chop around her neck to get the dog to play with her.

Yo' brother is so stupid, he sold the car for gas money.

Yo' daddy's glasses are so thick, when he looks at a map he sees people waving.

Yo' brother's hair is so greasy, when he gets in the car the oil light comes on.

Yo' mama is so short, you can see her feet on her driver's license.

Yo' daddy's head is so big, it shows up on radar.

Yo' sister is so skinny, her pajamas only have one stripe.

Yo' brother is so stupid, they had to burn the school down to get him out of third grade.

TOP 10 PRACTICAL JOKES, PART 1

Not for the faint of heart or soft of bottom (because if you try one of these, you'll probably get your butt kicked).

1. Weave a Web

Get a roll of transparent tape and make a web across a doorframe. Make sure that when you open the door, it opens *away* from the tape. Unless someone knows the tape is there, it will be hard to see. The next person who walks through the door will get stuck in the tape!

2. Toilet Roll Trick

Take a roll of toilet paper and unroll it. Then write some goofy messages on the sheets, like, "Help! I'm trapped in a toilet paper factory!" Roll it back up and put it on the holder. Then wait for a reaction.

3. The Glass of Water & the Pin

Get a glass of water and a pin. Tell your victim you can pin the glass of water to the wall using an ordinary straight pin. When they say, "Yeah, right," hold the glass up to the wall and start to pin it up...but then "accidentally" drop the pin. Now, holding the glass in position, ask your victim to pick up the pin for you. When he bends down to pick it up, dump the water on his head. Now run!

For Part 2 of the Top 10 Practical Jokes, turn to page 165.

KNOCK KNOCK JOKES

Knock-knock!
Who's there?
Lettuce.
Lettuce who?
Lettuce in and
you'll find out.

Knock-knock!
Who's there?
Woo.
Woo who?
Don't get so excited,
it's just a joke.

KNOCK-KNOCK!

WHO'S THERE?

canoe.

canoe WHO?

canoe COME OUT AND PLAY?

Two guys are out walking in the woods. The first guy says, "Did you see that?"

"No," the second guy says.

"Well, a bald eagle just flew overhead," the first guy says.

"Oh," says the second guy.

A couple of minutes later, the first guy says, "Did you see that?"

"See what?" the second guy asks.

"Are you blind? There was a big, black bear walking on that hill over there."

"Oh."

A few minutes later, the first guy says, "Did you see that?"

By now, the second guy is getting aggravated, so he says, "Yes, I did!"

And the first guy says: "Then why did you step in it?"

Why do bees have sticky hair?

Because they have honeycombs.

WHAT DO YOU CALL A COW THAT HAS JUST HAD A BABY?

DECALFINATED.

What do you say when someone throws a duck at a duck?
Duck, duck!

What do you say when someone throws a goose at a duck?
Duck, duck!
Goose.

What kind of car does Mickey Mouse's wife drive?

A Minnie van.

WHY DID THE TURTLE CROSS THE ROAD?

TO GET TO THE SHELL STATION.

What do get when you cross a rabbit with a spider?

A hare net.

Monster Jokes

What do you get if you cross a snowball with a werewolf?

Frostbite.

Why should vampires brush their fangs?

Because they have bat breath.

What has fur and flies?

A dead werewolf.

What do you get when you cross a vampire bat with a pygmy?

A little sucker.

What do witches put on their hair?

Scare spray.

Two skeletons used by an anatomy class were stowed away in a closet. After several weeks, one turned to the other and asked,

"What are we doing shut up in here, anyway?"

"Got me," admitted his companion. "If we had any guts, we'd bust out of here."

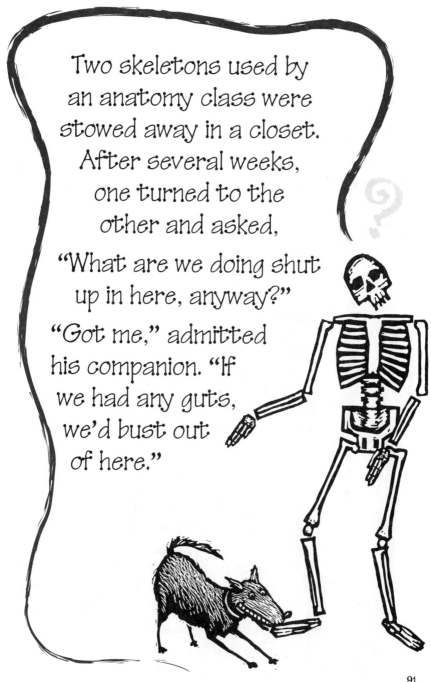

silly Science

EWW...SLIME

*This slime will stretch, snap, and break. You can
mold it, fold it, roll it up in a ball, and bounce it.
Leave some on a plate for an hour, and it'll get
flat and shiny. Here's how to make it.*

What You Need

- Plastic film canisters
- Jar with lid
- 1 measuring cup
- 2 teaspoons white glue (Elmer's)
- Bowl
- Spoon
- 1/2 cup warm water
- 1 teaspoon borax (you'll find it near the laundry detergent at the supermarket)

Preparation

Put the warm water and the borax together
in the jar. Close the lid and shake the mixture
until the borax dissolves. In a bowl, add the
2 teaspoons of water and the 2 teaspoons
of white glue. Mix really well. Add 1 teaspoon
of the borax solution to the glue mixture.

Keep mixing the slime for 3 to 5 minutes. It
will stiffen and be hard to mix but do it anyway! Kneading the slime is a very important
part of the process. To keep your slime
from drying out, store it in the film canisters.

You can use the rest of the borax solution
to make more slime—you might even want to
add a drop or two of food coloring while
you're kneading your second batch.

A SILLY SONG

Bug Juice

(Sung to the tune of "On Top of Old Smokey")

At camp with the Girl Scouts,
They gave us a drink;
We thought it was Kool-Aid
Because it was pink.

But the thing that they told us
Would have grossed out a moose,
For the good-tasting pink drink
Was really bug juice.

It looked fresh and fruity,
Like tasty Kool-Aid,
But the bugs that were in it,
Were murdered with Raid.

We drank by the gallon,
We drank by the ton,
But then the next morning,
We all had the runs.

Next time you drink bug juice,
And a fly drives you mad,
He's just getting even,
'Cause you swallowed his dad.

EGGS-TRAORDINARY STRENGTH!

Think you're strong? Try crushing an egg with your bare hand.

What You Need

- 1 egg, uncooked, with no cracks in the shell.
- 1 human (not wearing a ring) willing to test their strength.
- A sink—just in case there was a crack in the egg you didn't see (or the "willing human" happens to be Superman).

What You Do

Hold the egg lengthwise in the palm of one hand and squeeze really hard. Harder! Even harder! It can't be cracked with just your hand.

How It Works

The shape of the egg distributes pressure evenly over a large area. That's why cooks will always crack an egg on a hard surface first. They're applying pressure to a small spot to crack the egg.

One-Way Street

Skye, who was just learning to drive, went down a one-way street in the wrong direction, but she didn't break the law. How come?

Brain Teasers

Farm Hands

A dog named Rufus lived on a farm. Three other dogs lived on the farm, too. Their names were Blackie, Whitey, and Brownie. What do you think the fourth dog's name was?

Answers are on next page.

Chess Enigma

Clay and Caitlin played five games of chess. There were no ties in any of the games, yet each won the same number of games and lost the same number of games. How is that possible?

Solutions

Solutions

ANSWERS FOR BRAIN TEASERS ON PREVIOUS PAGE.

One-Way Street

Skye was walking.

Farm Hands

The fourth dog was named Rufus.

Chess Enigma

They weren't playing each other.

REAL PUNNY NAMES

Ever wish you had a different name? Imagine how you'd feel if you had one of these.

Doris Closed

Althea Thoon

Ella Vader

Dewey Care

Iona Carr

José Ken Eusee

Hanson Feet

Ewell B. Sorry

Dwayne Pipes

Bjorn Toulouse

Filmore Payne

Ellie Funt

Warren Peace

Annie More

Harley Worthit

Faye Tallity

Earl E. Byrd

Rhoda Mule

Hans R. Dirty

Armand A. Legg

Fred F. DeDark

Harrison Fire

A TRUE STORY

A man named Terry Romine went into a convenience store in West Virginia and ordered a slice of pizza. But instead of paying, he told the clerk he had a gun and wanted all the cash in the register. The clerk had trouble opening the cash register, so Romine grabbed the whole thing and ran out.

Then the clerk looked down and saw that the robber had left his wallet (containing his driver's license) on the counter. Police had no difficulty locating—and arresting—Romine.

SAY IT, DON'T SPRAY IT

A tongue twister.

Did You Eever Iver Ever

In your leaf loaf life

See the deevil divil devil

Kiss his weef wofe wife?

No, I neever niver never

In my leaf loaf life

Saw the deevil divil devil

Kiss his weef wofe wife.

GAMES

STICK TO THE CHAIR

Tell your friends that, using only the power of your pointer finger, you will make it impossible for them to stand up.

What You Need:
One firm straight-backed chair and one friend who's willing to be subjected to your all-powerful pointer finger.

What You Do:
Have your victim—er—friend sit in the chair with both feet on the floor next to each other. (No slouching—your friend needs to sit up nice and straight.) Supercharge your pointer finger by blowing on it, then place it in the middle of your friend's forehead and press lightly. Challenge your friend to stand up, without using her hands and without bending her back. She can't!

How It Works:
Just the light pressure of your finger on her forehead stops her from using the weight of her upper body as leverage to stand up. To stand without using her hands, she needs to lean her upper body over her feet.

1 Minute Mystery

THE SULTAN'S SECRET

Ali Baba has decided to steal the sultan's treasure. In the dead of night, he slips past the palace guards and makes his way through a maze of tunnels to a room with two doors. The sultan's daughter told Ali that a chest filled with jewels and gold lies behind one of the doors. Behind the other door is a hungry lion. But Ali doesn't know which door is which.

Two guards stand beside the doors. The sultan's daughter also warned Ali that one of the guards always tells the truth, while the other one always lies. Both of them know what lies behind each door but Ali has no way of knowing which is the honest guard and which is the liar. He is allowed to ask one of the guards one question. What should he ask in order to be certain that he will open the right door?

You'll find the answer on the next page.

Solution

THE SULTAN'S SECRET

There are two possible answers for the puzzle on the previous page.

Answer 1. Ali asks one guard what the other guard would say if asked which door leads to the treasure. Ali should open the *other* door.

Answer 2. Ali asks one guard what the other guard would say if he asked him which door leads to the hungry lion. In this case, Ali should open *this door.*

FUNNY ANSWERING MACHINE MESSAGES

Hi. I'm probably home. I'm just avoiding someone I don't like. Leave me a message, and if I don't call back, it's you.

We're not home,
we're rarely home,
And when we're home,
We're on the phone,
So please leave a message at the tone!

Hello, this is Sally's microwave. Her answering machine just eloped with her DVD player, so I'm stuck taking her calls. If you want anything cooked while you leave your message, just hold it up to the phone.

You've reached Alpha Centauri Space Station. Commander Marlin can't come to the phone right now. He's either saving the universe from some dreaded, nameless peril—or perhaps he's taking a nappie. Leave your name and number after the beep, and he will return your call.

CLASSIC RIDDLES

I am always hungry,
I must always be fed,
The finger I lick
Will soon turn red.
  What am I?

You heard me before,
Yet you hear me again,
Then I die,
'Till you call me again.
  What am I?

An echo

You can see nothing else
When you look in my
  face.
I will look you in the
  eye
And I will never lie.
  What am I?

Your reflection

I build up castles.
I tear down
  mountains.
I make some men
  blind,
I help others to see.
  What am I?

Sand

Weight in my belly,
Trees on my back,
Nails in my ribs,
Feet I do lack.
  What am I?

A ship

Until I am measured
I am not known,
Yet how you miss me
When I have flown.
  What am I?

Time

????

LAST LAUGHS: EPITAPHS

An epitaph is an inscription on a tombstone. These real epitaphs prove that death isn't all seriousness.

On Beza Wood's grave in Winslow, Maine:

Here lies one Wood
Enclosed in wood.
One Wood
Within another.
The outer wood
Is very good:
We cannot praise
The other.

In Albany, New York:

Looked up the elevator shaft to see if the car was on the way down. It was.

In THURMONT, MARYLAND:
Here lies an atheist
all dressed up
and no place to go.

Anna Hopewell's grave in
Enosburg Falls, Vermont:

Here lies the body of our Anna
Done to death by a banana.
It wasn't the fruit that laid her low
But the skin of the thing that made her go.

MATH-MAGICAL

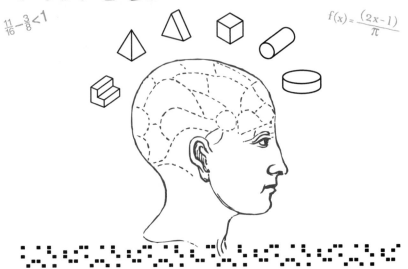

$\frac{11}{16} - \frac{3}{8} < 1$

$f(x) = \dfrac{(2x-1)}{\pi}$

GIMME 5!

This is crazy, but it works.

1. Ask a friend to pick any number.

2. Add the next higher number to it.

3. Add 9.

4. Divide by 2.

5. Subtract the original number.

6. What'd you get?

Is the answer 5? You bet it is!

YOU'RE GROUNDED

MAKE YOUR OWN WHOOPEE CUSHION

What every kid needs to know to make one of the classic prank toys of all time!

What You Need

- 1 latex balloon
- 1 Popsicle stick
- 1 unsuspecting victim

- Any chair or couch that has a removable cushion

Preparation

1. Wedge the Popsicle stick across the inside of the neck of the balloon. (This will take some work, but you should be able to do it.)

2. Blow 4 or 5 times into the balloon—don't tie off the balloon, the Popsicle stick will stretch the neck of the balloon tight enough so the air won't easily escape

3. Just before your victim goes to sit in their favorite chair, place your whoopee cushion underneath the chair cushion...and wait.

ELEPHANT JOKES

What's the difference between an elephant and an egg?

If you don't know, I hope you don't do the grocery shopping!

What's the difference between an African elephant and an Indian elephant?

About 3,000 miles.

Why did the elephant sit on the marshmallow?

So she wouldn't fall into the hot chocolate.

What's the difference between an elephant and a flea?

An elephant can have fleas, but a flea can't have elephants.

WHY ARE ELEPHANTS LARGE, GRAY, AND WRINKLED?

BECAUSE IF THEY WERE SMALL, WHITE, AND SMOOTH, THEY WOULD BE ASPIRINS.

How do you tell if there's an elephant in your refrigerator?
Look for his footprints in the cheesecake.

How do you tell if there are two elephants in your refrigerator?
Look for two sets of footprints in the cheesecake.

How do you tell if there are three elephants in your refrigerator?
The door won't close.

How many giraffes will fit in the refrigerator?
None. There are already too many elephants in there.

How do you get an elephant into a Volkswagen Beetle?
Open door, insert elephant, close door.

How do you get four elephants into a Volkswagen?
Two in the front, two in the back.

How do you know if an elephant is visiting your house?
There's a Volkswagen parked outside with three elephants in it.

How do you get eight elephants in a refrigerator?
Put four elephants in one Volkswagen, put four elephants in another Volkswagen, and put the two Volkswagens in the refrigerator.

But two Volkswagens won't fit in a refrigerator.
There were two elephants in there, and a Volkswagen isn't as big as an elephant!

DID YOU KNOW?

IT TAKES 4 HOURS TO HARD-BOIL AN OSTRICH EGG.

The largest animal on earth is the blue whale. It's tongue is bigger than an elephant. It's heart is as big as a car!

If you had the jumping power of a flea, you would be able to jump over a 70-story building.

THERE ARE NO TIGERS IN AFRICA.

It is possible for a fish to get seasick.

In sky-writing, the average letter is two miles high.

What do you call a boy
hanging on the wall?
Art.

Did you hear about
the cat that swallowed
a ball of wool?
She had mittens!

Justin: "Teacher, would
you punish me for some-
thing I didn't do?"
Teacher: "Of course not,
Justin."
Justin: "Good. Because I
didn't do my homework."

HOW DO YOU BEGIN
A FLEA RACE?
JUST SAY, "ONE,
TWO, FLEA--GO!"

Jokes

Why was
Cinderella such
a terrible soccer
player?
She had a pumpkin
for a coach.

Jokes

Teacher: "Timmy, go
to the map and find
North America."

Timmy: "Here it is."

Teacher: "That is
correct. Now, class,
who discovered
North America?"

Class: "Timmy!"

Jokes

Little Red Riding Hood was skipping down the road when she saw the Big Bad Wolf crouched down behind a log. "My, what big eyes you have, Mr. Wolf," said Little Red Riding Hood. The surprised wolf jumped up and ran away.

Farther down the road, Little Red Riding Hood saw the wolf again; this time he was crouched behind a tree stump. "My, what big ears you have, Mr. Wolf," she said. Again the foiled wolf jumped up and ran away.

About two miles down the road, Little Red Riding Hood saw the wolf again, this time crouched down behind a road sign. "My, what big teeth you have, Mr. Wolf," taunted Little Red Riding Hood.

With that the Big Bad Wolf jumped up and screamed, "Will you get lost? I'm trying to go to the bathroom!"

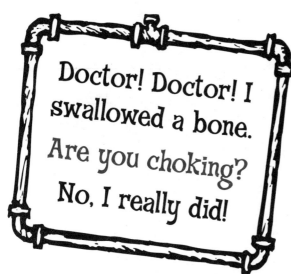

Doctor! Doctor! I swallowed a bone.

Are you choking?

No, I really did!

DOCTOR! DOCTOR! HOW DO I STOP MY NOSE FROM RUNNING?

STICK YOUR FOOT OUT AND TRIP IT UP!

Doctor! Doctor! These pills you gave me for B.O....

What's wrong with them?

They keep slipping out from under my arms!

Doctor! Doctor! I think I'm suffering from déjà vu!

Didn't I see you yesterday?

113

One afternoon in a beginner's skydiving class, the students sat attentively as the instructor lectured. At the end of the class she asked if anyone had any questions.

Somebody asked, "If the parachute doesn't open, and the reserve chute doesn't open, how long do we have until we hit the ground?"

The instructor looked at her and answered, "The rest of your life."

FATHER & SON

Another puzzle to challenge your brain. (Answer on next page.)

Bill recently celebrated his birthday.

"I just noticed something," Bill said to his son, Bill Jr. "If you add my age to yours, the sum is 66."

"Not only that," said Bill Jr., "but your age is my age reversed."

How old are they? (There are three possible solutions.)

Solution

Answers from the previous page.

FATHER & SON

• If Bill is 51,
Bill Jr. would be 15.

• If Bill is 42,
Bill Jr. would be 24.

• If Bill is 60,
Bill Jr. would be (0)6.

How is the
letter T like
an island?
It's always
in the middle
of water.

Did you
hear about the two
morons that froze
to death at the
drive-in?

*They went
to see "Closed
for Winter."*

WHAT LIES AT
THE BOTTOM OF
THE OCEAN AND
TWITCHES?
A NERVOUS
WRECK.

What did one
flea say to the
other flea?

*"Should we
walk, or take
the dog?"*

Three kids—Paul, Mark, and Dash—are on the ground while three soldiers are flying overhead in an airplane. The first soldier takes a bite out of an apple and says, "This apple is rotten!" and throws it out the window.

The second man takes a bite out of an orange and says, "This orange is sour!" and throws it out the window.

The third guy gets a grenade and pulls the clip and says, "Must be a dud!" and throws it out the window.

On the ground Paul and Mark are crying and Dash is laughing. Giggling uncontrollably, Dash asks Paul, "Why are you crying?"

Paul answers, "An apple fell out of the sky and hit me on the head."

Dash, still laughing, asks Mark, "Why are you crying?"

"An orange fell out of thin air and hit me on the head."

When Dash nearly falls over laughing, both Paul and Mark ask him what's so funny. He says, "I just farted, and that building blew up."

Who won the skeleton beauty contest?

No body.

What do skeletons say before they begin dining?

"Bone appétit!"

When do ghosts usually appear?

Just before someone screams.

The famous Olympic skier Picabo (pronounced "Peek-A-Boo") Street is also a nurse. She currently works at the Intensive Care Unit of a large metropolitan hospital.

She is not permitted to answer the telephone, however, as it caused simply too much confusion when she would answer the phone and say, "Picabo, ICU."

Jokes

Ho Ho!

What has a bottom at the top? Your legs.

HA!

Tee Hee...

Tee Hee...

What's a mosquito's favorite sport?

Skin diving!

Yuk!

Yuk!

Why is a stadium the coolest place?

Because of all the fans in the stands.

Yuk!

Ho Ho!

Tee Hee...

Yuk!

Tee Hee...

HA!

chortle...

Tee Hee...

chortle...

What did Geronimo say when he jumped out of the airplane?
ME!!!

Ho Ho!

Yuk!

chortle...

Yuk!
HA!

Ho Ho!

HO HO!

How do you close an envelope underwater?

With a seal.

Tiger: I always carry a spare pair of pants with me when I golf.

Ernie: Why?

Tiger: I might get a hole-in-one.

YUK!

HA!

Ho Ho!

HA!

YUK!

Ha!

HA!

TeeHee...

chortle...

*T*he mayor wanted to get more townspeople to attend the city council meetings. One council member suggested bringing in a hypnotist. Everyone thought it was a great idea.

A few weeks later, the town hall was packed, and the townspeople sat fascinated as the hypnotist took out a pocket watch and began to chant, "Watch the watch, watch the watch, watch the watch..."

The crowd grew mesmerized as the watch swayed back and forth, back and forth, back and forth...

Suddenly the hypnotist's fingers slipped and the watch fell to the floor.

"Crap!" said the hypnotist.

It took three weeks to clean up the town hall.

Two Eskimos in a kayak
got really cold, but when they
lit a fire in the craft, it sank,
proving once and for all that
you can't have your kayak
and heat it, too.

Which is the
fastest, cold
or heat?

Heat—you can
catch a cold.

WHAT ALWAYS
FALLS WITHOUT
GETTING HURT?
RAIN.

What do you give
an injured lemon?

Lemonade.

HOW DO YOU STOP FISH
FROM SMELLING?
CUT THEIR NOSES OFF.

MAGIC

IT'S KNOT POSSIBLE!

*Dare a friend to tie a knot in a piece of
rope without letting go of the ends. He
won't be able to do it—but you will!*

What You Need

1 piece of rope,
   3 or 4 feet long

The Setup

Have your friend hold the rope as in the picture
below. Let him try to tie a knot without letting go
of either end at any time. When he gives up, take
the rope back and lay it down on a table.

The Trick

Cross your arms before
you pick up the rope.
Pick up one end at a time
to make it easier to grasp.

When you uncross your arms, a knot will appear in the
middle of the rope—but you haven't let go of either end.

LAST LAUGH: EPITAPHS

In London:
Here lies Ann Mann.
She lived an old maid
But died an old Mann.

In Nova Scotia, Canada:
Here lies
Ezekial
Aikle
Age 102
The good
die young.

In Ribbesford, England:
The children of Israel wanted bread
And the Lord sent them manna.
Old clerk Wallace wanted a wife,
And the Devil sent him Anna.

the Graffiti Page

"Is this chicken or is this fish? I know it's tuna. But it says chicken. By the sea."
—Jessica Simpson

Does killing time damage eternity?

Birdie, birdie in the sky
Dropped some white
    stuff in my eye.
I'm a big girl, I won't cry,
I'm just glad that cows don't fly.

If at first you don't succeed… losing may just be your style!

is a SLEEPING BULL a BULLDOZER?

Can you help me out?

Which way did you come in?

DON'T LOSE ANY SLEEP OVER INSOMNIA.

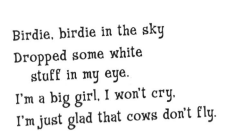

IS THAT A FLYING SAUCER OR A PIE IN THE SKY?

See a pin, pick it up. All the day you'll have…a pin.

YOU NAME IT

FUNNY TOWN NAMES

*Here are some stories of how
towns got their weird names.*

Spot, Tennessee

One day, pen in hand, the operator of the town sawmill sat at his desk, worrying over a letter from postal authorities who wanted to know what to call the unnamed town. A spot of ink dropped onto the piece of white paper—and the town had its name.

Chicken, Alaska

The miners who founded this town lived off *ptarmigan*, a type of bird that from far away looks like a chicken. They wanted to name the town after their favorite fowl, but ptarmigan was just too hard to spell.

Hell, Michigan

When settlers got together to name the town in 1841, they argued so much that finally one of them had enough. "You can name it Hell if you want to!" he yelled, and stomped out. The name stuck.

Why Not, North Carolina

At an 1860 meeting, residents were trying to come up with a name for their town. People kept saying, "Why not name it this. Why not name it that." Finally someone asked, "Why not name it Why Not?" So they did.

Toad Suck, Arkansas

This place was a steamboat landing in the 19th century. The captains and crewmen were said to suck down so much whisky in the local saloon that they "swole up like toads."

STEP THROUGH A POSTCARD

This a totally cool trick that will blow your friends' socks off. Follow the instructions to the letter...

What You Need: A postcard and a pair of scissors

1. Fold the postcard in half lengthwise.

2. Use the scissors to cut a horizontal slit

Fig. 1

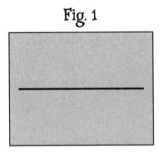

along the crease, stopping about 1/4 inch from each edge (Fig. 1).

3. Start about 1/4 inch from the end of the postcard and carefully cut a vertical slit across the folded edge.

4. Continue cutting slits across the postcard until you have reached the other end. Be careful not to cut the card all the way through.

Fig. 2

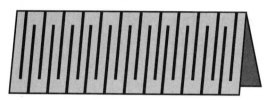

5. Now, turn the postcard over and cut from the other side. Again, be sure not to cut all the way through (Fig. 2).

6. Gently open up the card. It will look like (Fig. 3).

Fig. 3

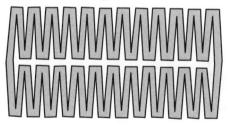

7. Open it out still farther. It will unfold into a long accordion strip that you'll be able to step through easily.

There was once an aspiring veterinarian who put himself through veterinary school working nights as a taxidermist. When he graduated he decided he could combine his two occupations to better serve the needs of his patients and their owners, while doubling his practice and, therefore, his income. He opened his own office with a sign on the door saying:

Dr. Smith,
Veterinary Medicine
and Taxidermy:
Either way, you get
your dog back!

Charlie was practicing the violin in the living room while his father was trying to read in the den. The family dog was lying in the den, and when the screeching sounds of the violin reached his ears, he began to howl loudly.

The father listened to the dog and the violin as long as he could. Then he jumped up, slammed his paper to the floor, and yelled above the noise, "For goodness' sake, Charlie, can't you play something the dog doesn't know?"

Gross Jokes

Q: When do cannibals leave the table?

A: *When everyone's eaten.*

Q: What is Beethoven doing in his grave?

A: *Decomposing!*

Q: Why did the boy bring toilet paper to the birthday party?

A: *Because he was a party pooper!*

Q: What do you call a guy who was born in New York, married in Florida, and died in Ohio?

A: *Dead!*

Q: What's the difference between boogers and broccoli?

A: *Kids don't eat broccoli!*

Q: Did you hear about the Indian chief who drank 15 cups of tea before bedtime?

A: *That night he drowned in his tea-pee!*

Q: Where do you find a no-legged dog?

A: *Right where you left him.*

Phh-art

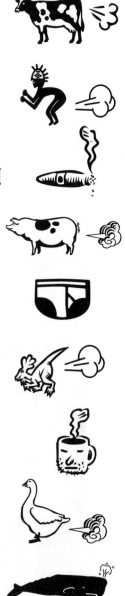

An old lady was riding the elevator in a high-rise apartment building when a beautiful young woman got in, smelling of expensive perfume. She turned to the old woman and said arrogantly, "Romance by Ralph Lauren, $150 an ounce!"

Another beautiful young woman, also reeking of expensive perfume, got on the elevator, and declared snottily, "Chanel No. 5, $200 an ounce!"

The elevator came to the old lady's floor, but before she got off, she turned and ripped a thunderous fart. "Broccoli," she snapped. "49 cents a pound!"

Silly Science

OOZE

*Gross out your parents
and impress your friends by
making your own slimy toy.*

What You Need
- Mixing bowl
- 1 cup cornstarch
- Food coloring
- 1/2 cup water

Preparation

Put the cornstarch in the bowl
and add a drop or two of food coloring. Slowly add the water, mixing the
cornstarch and water with your fingers
until the powder is wet.

Keep gradually mixing in water until
the Ooze feels wet like a liquid. Then
try tapping on the surface of it with
your finger or a spoon. When the Ooze
is just right, it won't splash—it will feel
solid. If your Ooze is too powdery, add a
little more water. If it's too wet, add
more cornstarch.

EWW...THERE'S CHOCOLATE IN MY DIAPER!

*Here's a game that's sure
to gross everyone out.*

What You Need

· A group of friends.

· Disposable diapers—the same number as there are
people in the group.

· Candy bars—the same number. (Choose a different
one for each diaper: Snickers, Tootsie Rolls, Almond
Joy—whatever you like.)

· A microwave oven.

Setup

1. Have your friends sit in the living room while you
prepare the diapers.

2. Unwrap the candy bars and place one in each
diaper.

3. Make sure you mark the diapers in some way so
you remember which diaper has which candy bar. For

example: Mark them A, B, C, etc., then list the letters and corresponding candy on a piece of paper.

4. Microwave each diaper (with the candy bar in it) for 30 to 45 seconds.

5. When all the diapers are heated and the "candy poo" is ready to serve, carry them out on a tray, along with paper and pens for everyone.

How To Play

1. Pass the diapers around the circle.

2. Each player has to sniff each diaper and guess what brand of chocolatey poo is in it—then write it down.

3. When everyone has had a chance to sniff them all, read off the correct answers.

4. The winner is the player with the most correct guesses!

The Prize

The winner gets the poopy diaper of their choice and gets to eat it right out of the diaper! The rest of the players get to fight over the remaining diapers and their contents.

Don't Forget the Camera!

Photos of players licking diapers with brown smears all over their faces are...well...pretty disgusting.

A TRUE STORY

Police in Winnipeg, caught a man trying to steal a car from a parking lot. They didn't have to go far to find the suspect— he was trying to steal it from the police parking lot.

LAST LAUGH: EPITAPHS

In Ruidoso,
New Mexico:

Here lies
Johnny Yeast
Pardon me
For not rising.

From Boot Hill in Tombstone, Arizona:

Here lies Lester Moore

Four slugs from a .44

No Les No More.

MATH-MAGICAL

$\frac{11}{16} - \frac{3}{8} < 1$

$f(x) = \frac{(2x-1)}{\pi}$

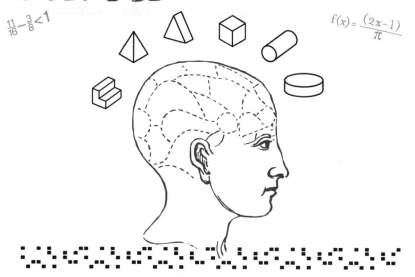

CHECK IT OUT

*Here's some more fun you can have
with a calculator and numbers.*

1. Pick a secret number from 1 to 9.

2. Multiply that number by 9.

3. Multiply that number by 123,456,789.

*The answer will be your secret number,
repeated in a row with one stray 0 thrown in.*

EXAMPLE: If your number is 7, multiply it by 9
(7 x 9 = 63). Now multiply 63 by 123,456,789.
You will get: 7777777707. Amazing!

One day, a bunch of animals were sitting around, bored. Suddenly, the lion had an idea. "I know a really exciting game called football. I've seen the humans play it on TV."

He proceeded to describe it to the rest of the animals. They all got excited about it and decided to play. They went out to a field, chose up teams, and were ready to begin.

The lion's team was able to get two first downs, but then had to punt. The mule punted. The rhino was back deep for the kick. He caught the ball, lowered his head, and charged. First, he ran over a roadrunner, then stepped on two rabbits. He gored a wildebeest, knocked over two cows, and scored a touchdown.

Unfortunately, they lacked a placekicker, so the score remained 6-0.

Late in the first half, the lion's team scored a touchdown and the mule kicked the extra point. The lion's team led at halftime 7-6. In the locker room, the lion gave a pep talk.

"Look, you guys. We've got the lead and we can win this game. They only have one real threat: the rhino. Mule, when you kick off make sure you keep it away from the rhino."

The second half began. Just as the mule was about to kick off, the rhino's team changed formation and the ball went directly to the rhino. Once again, he lowered his head and was off running. First, he stomped two gazelles. He skewered a zebra and bulldozed an elephant. It looked like he was home free. Suddenly at the 20-yard line, he dropped to the ground. It looked like there were no other animals anywhere near him, so the lion went over to see what had happened. Right next to the fallen rhino he saw a small centipede.

"Did you do this?" he asked the centipede.

"Yeah," the centipede replied.

The lion retorted, "We could have used you during the first half. Where were you?"

"I was putting on my shoes."

FUNNY ANSWERING MACHINE MESSAGES

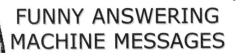

This is you-know-who.
We are you-know-where.
Leave your you-know-
what you-know-when.

BEEP

I'm here in spirit only at the
moment, but if you'll leave
your name and number, I'll
get back to you as soon as
I'm here in person.

Now I lay me down to sleep;
Leave a message at the beep.
If I should die before I wake,
Remember to erase the tape.

Q: Why do hummingbirds hum?
A: Because they can't remember the words.

Q: What do you call a very old ant?
A: An antique.

Q: What would you get if you crossed a sweet potato with a jazz band?
A: A yam session.

Q: Why do seagulls
fly over the sea?
A: If they flew over the bay,
they'd be bagels.

What do you
call a cat that falls
into a trashcan?
Kitty litter!

WHY DO CATS
EAT FUR BALLS?
BECAUSE THEY
LOVE A GOOD GAG!

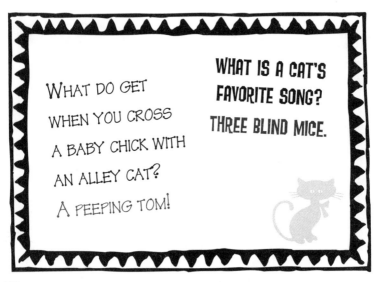

WHAT DO GET
WHEN YOU CROSS
A BABY CHICK WITH
AN ALLEY CAT?
A PEEPING TOM!

WHAT IS A CAT'S
FAVORITE SONG?
THREE BLIND MICE.

the Graffiti Page

Operations are funny. They leave you in stitches!

When night falls, who picks it up?

To make your dreams come true, stay awake.

GOD GIVE ME PATIENCE...AND DO IT RIGHT NOW!

GOBLIN YOUR FOOD IS BAD FOR YOUR ELF!

CAN FAT PEOPLE GO SKINNY-DIPPING?

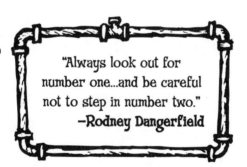

"Always look out for number one...and be careful not to step in number two."
—Rodney Dangerfield

WHY DO YOUR FEET SMELL BUT YOUR NOSE RUNS?

Give him an inch and he thinks he's a ruler.

EYE-EYE CAPTAIN

Fred was interviewing the pirate Peg-Legged Pete...

Fred: So, Pete, how did you lose your leg?

Pete: A cannon blew off my leg in a fierce battle.

Fred: And how did you lose your hand?

Pete: Same battle.

Fred: Then what happened to your eye? Surely you didn't lose that in a battle as well?

Pete: Oh, no. I was on the deck of my ship when a seagull pooped in my eye.

Fred: Seagull poop knocked out your eye?

Pete: No. It was the first day I had my hook.

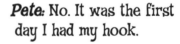

LIMERICKS

Here's another batch of Uncle John's favorite limericks.

A silly young man from Clyde

In a funeral procession was spied;

When asked, "Who is dead?"

He giggled and said,

"I don't know; I just came for the ride."

There was a young woman named Bright,

Whose speed was much faster than light,

She set out one day

In a relative way,

And returned on the previous night.

There was a young person called Smarty,
Who sent out some cards for a party;
So exclusive and few
Were the friends that he knew
That no one was present but Smarty.

Bobby
was making
faces at the
other kids on
the playground,
so his teacher
decided to have
a word with him.

"Bobby, when I was
a child," she said gently,
"I was told that if I made
an ugly face, it would freeze
and I would stay like that."

Bobby looked up
at her sweetly.
"Well, Ms.
Smith," he
remarked, "you can't
say you weren't warned."

Jokes & Puns !

Ho Ho !

Tee Hee...

Ho Ho !

A lonely frog goes to a fortune-teller to find out what his future holds. The fortune-teller says, "You are going to meet a beautiful young girl who will want to know everything about you."

Ho Ho !

The frog is thrilled. "This is great! Where will I meet her, at work or at a party?"

"In a biology class."

HA !   Tee Hee...   chortle...   HA !   Tee Hee...   chortle...

Tee Hee...   Ho Ho !   Yuk !

chortle...

Yuk !
HA !

This was overheard when the police were investigating the murder of Juan Gonzalez:

YUK !

"It looks like he was shot with a golf gun," one detective said.

HA !

Ho Ho !

HO HO !

"A golf gun?" said the chief of police. "What in the world is a golf gun?"

Ho Ho !

HA !

"I don't know. But it sure made a hole in Juan."

YUK !

HA !

Ha !

TeeHee...

chortle...

A Bird Joke

One day a man went to an auction and made a bid on a parrot. He really wanted the bird but kept getting outbid. So he bid higher...and higher...and higher. Even though he had to bid way more than he intended, he finally won the bird! As he was paying for it, he said to the auctioneer,

"I sure hope this parrot can talk. I'd hate to have paid this much to find out that he can't!"

"Don't worry," replied the auctioneer. "Who do you think kept bidding against you?"

A guy opens his door and finds a snail at his doorstep. He picks up the snail and hurls it across the front lawn.

Two years later, there's a knock at the door. The guy opens the door and there's the snail, who asks, "Hey, what was that all about?"

Two cows are standing in a field. One says to the other, "I'm worried about this mad cow disease. Are you?"

The other cow laughs. "Why should I care? I'm a helicopter."

LOST DOG: 3 legs,
blind in one eye,
missing right ear,
tail broken,
recently neutered.
Answers to the
name of "Lucky."

LOOK SMART!

More weird facts.

• In Bladworth, Saskatchewan, it's illegal to frown at cows.

• Our eyes stay the same size from birth, but our noses and ears never stop growing.

• Bullfrogs can swallow each other whole.

• Over 50% of the people in the world have never made or received a phone call.

• In Canada it's illegal to pay for a 50-cent item with only pennies.

• A vest made of fabric woven from spiderweb silk would be bulletproof.

• When Albert Einstein thought his pet parrot was depressed, he did what any normal genius would do—he told it parrot jokes to cheer it up.

This guy goes to a costume party with a girl on his back.

"What the heck are you?" asks the host.

"I'm a snail," says the guy.

"But...you have a girl on your back," replies the host.

"Yeah," he says. "That's Michelle."

1 Minute Mystery

WALKING IN THE RAIN

Rita, Vera, Chuck, and Dave arrive at a friend's house for a party. It's raining and no one wants to get soaked walking from the car to the house. But they have only one umbrella. They decide to have Chuck, the fastest, walk each person into the house, then return to get the next person. It takes Chuck one minute to walk each way, Rita 2 minutes, Dave 5 minutes, and Vera 10 minutes, so it should take a total of 19 minutes to get all of them into the party. But Vera says she knows a way they can all get into the house in only 17 minutes.

How?

(Remember, they have to use the umbrella to get to and from the house, and only two of them can go at a time.)

You'll find the answer on the next page.

Solution

WALKING
IN THE RAIN

Answers for previous page

There are two possible answers to this puzzle.

Answer 1:

Chuck and Rita walk together to the house (2 minutes), and Chuck returns with the umbrella (1 minute). Dave and Vera walk to the house (10 minutes), and Rita returns with the umbrella (2 minutes). Chuck and Rita walk to the house again (2 minutes). Total: 17 minutes.

Answer 2:

Chuck and Rita walk together to the house (2 minutes), and Rita returns with the umbrella (2 minutes). Dave and Vera walk to the house (10 minutes), and Chuck returns with the umbrella (1 minute). Chuck and Rita walk to the house again (2 minutes). Total: 17 minutes.

Monster Jokes

What kind of ship does Dracula captain?

A blood vessel.

WHAT KIND OF MONSTER IS SAFE TO PUT IN THE WASHING MACHINE?

A WASH-AND-WEAR WOLF.

WHAT DO YOU CALL A HAUNTED CHICKEN?

A POULTRY-GEIST.

What do you get when you cross a snowman with a vampire?

Frostbite.

DID YOU KNOW?

Amazing facts to tell your friends.

Flamingos can only eat with their heads upside down.

Some male spiders pluck their webs like a guitar to attract female spiders.

CROCODILES CAN'T STICK OUT THEIR TONGUES.

If you have three quarters, four dimes, and four pennies, you have $1.19. You also have the largest amount of money in coins without being able to make change for a dollar.

KNOCK KNOCK JOKES

Knock-knock!

Who's there?

Little old lady.

Little old lady who?

Nice yodeling!

Knock-knock!

Who's there?

Sara.

Sara who?

Sara doctor in the house? I'm sick.

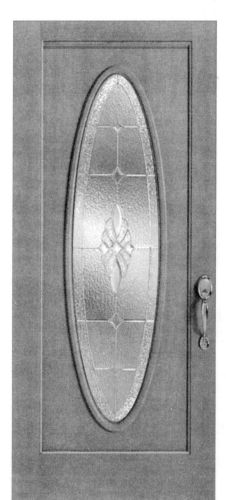

MATH WIZARD

*Here's a trick you can play on your friends
to show them what a math genius you
are. You are a math genius, right?*

Tell a friend that the two of you will take
turns picking five 5-digit numbers at random,
and then you'll add them together—but you,
the genius, will predict the sum of those five
numbers after seeing only the first number!

The Trick

• Your friend goes first. Have her write down
a 5-digit number. Note: The first digit cannot
be "9." For example, she might write 67,812.

• On a separate piece of paper, you will immediately write down the final "answer"
to this quiz (the total of all five 5-digit numbers), even though four haven't even been
selected yet!

• Announce that you have "predicted" the final
answer and written it down as proof—but don't
show it yet. Fold the piece of paper to keep the
answer hidden until the end of the "trick."

• Now have your friend write down a second 5-digit number directly beneath the first one.

• Quickly write down a third 5-digit number right below hers. (Aha! You'll have to know *what* to write. To find out, read the instructions below.)

• Next, have your friend write a fourth 5-digit number under your number. You immediately write a fifth 5-digit number beneath it. (Again, select that number according to the instructions below.)

• Now have your friend add up the five numbers.

• Compare that answer to the one you wrote down after the first number was selected. *They will be identical!* But how could you do that? How could you predict the total after just hearing the first number? Simply follow the instructions below.

How It Works

a. Take the first number and subtract 2 from it, then put the number "2" in front of it. For example, if the number was 67,812, it would be 267,810. (That will be the final answer.)

b. When you see the second number your friend writes down, mentally subtract each digit from 9, and write that answer as the third number. For example, if your friend's second number is 11,111, then the number you write down would be 88,888. Or, if your friend's number is 56,123, then your next number would be 43,876. The key here is that each of your friend's number's digits, when added to the corresponding digit of your number, must total 9.

c. Then ask your friend to write down a fourth number. Once again you subtract each digit of that number from 9 (do this silently) and write that answer down as the fifth number. For example, if the second number is 12,345, then you would write 87,654 as the third number (because 12,345 + 87,654 = 99,999).

d. When the five numbers the two of you have selected are all added together, the total will be identical to the number you originally wrote down and set aside. This works every time. Try it and see!

Jokes

Doctor! Doctor! I've lost my memory!

When did you lose it?

When did I lose what?

How do crazy people go through the forest?

They take the psycho path.

HOW MANY SPANIARDS DOES IT TAKE TO CHANGE A LIGHTBULB?

JUST JUAN.

HOW DID THE BUTCHER introduce HIS WIFE?

"MEET PATTY."

WHY COULDN'T THE SESAME SEED LEAVE THE GAMBLING CASINO?

BECAUSE HE WAS ON A ROLL.

phh-art (Part 1)

FUN FART FACTS

Because you can never know too much about the gas you pass...

• Farts travel at a speed of 10 feet per second.

• Cockroaches fart every 15 minutes.

• The Yanomami people of South America fart to say hello.

• A burglar hiding in a closet was caught because he gave himself away when he tooted his own horn.

• A doctor removing hemorrhoids had his eyebrows burned off when a fart caught fire.

• Who are the biggest farters on Earth? Termites. These insects produce about 20 million tons of gas a year—as much as all cars and factories put together!

Phh-art (Part 2)

THE FART THAT MADE A PHARAOH

I n 568 B.C., Pharaoh Apries of Egypt sent his best general, Ahmose, to put down a mutiny in his army. But the general joined the rebels instead.

So the pharaoh sent a messenger to tell the general to give up or else. General Ahmose replied by standing up in his saddle and farting. "Take that back to Apries," he told the messenger, who did as he was told.

The angry pharaoh cut off the messenger's nose and ears. That their ruler could be so cruel to his own messenger infuriated the Egyptian people. They sided with the general, who attacked the pharaoh's army and won. He became Pharaoh Ahmose and ruled for 44 years.

HOW INSULTING!

YO' DADDY'S SO BALD, YOU CAN
SEE WHAT'S ON HIS MIND.

YO' SISTER IS SO UGLY, HER DENTIST
TREATS HER BY MAIL ORDER.

YO' BROTHER IS SO STUPID, WHEN I ASKED
HIM IF HE WANTED TO PLAY ONE ON ONE,
HE SAID, "OKAY, BUT WHAT ARE THE TEAMS?"

YO' MAMA IS SO FAT, WHEN SHE GOES IN A RESTAU-
RANT, SHE LOOKS AT THE MENU AND SAYS, "OKAY."

YO' DADDY IS SO OLD, HE CALLED THE COPS
WHEN DAVID AND GOLIATH STARTED TO FIGHT.

YO' MAMA IS SO FAT, WHEN SHE FELL OVER, SHE
ROCKED HERSELF TO SLEEP TRYING TO GET UP AGAIN.

YO' SISTER IS SO UGLY, WHEN SHE'S AT
THE BEACH, CATS TRY TO BURY HER.

YO' BROTHER'S FEET ARE SO BIG, HIS
SHOES HAVE LICENSE PLATES.

Insults

YO' DADDY IS SO OLD...

- ...he was a waiter at the Last Supper.

- ...he knew Burger King when he was just a prince.

- ...his birth certificate expired.

- ...he has Adam and Eve's autographs.

- ...his Social Security number is 1.

- ...he got the first copy of the Ten Commandments.

- ...his memory is in black and white.

- ...when Moses split the Red Sea, he was on the other side fishing.

- ...when we told him to act his age, he died.

You're Grounded

MORE PRANKS

If you play one of these dirty tricks on someone, you'll soon be spending a lot of quality time alone in your room...

REMOTE MADNESS

If you can see your intended victim's TV through a window, you can do this prank. Get a universal TV remote. Find out what brand of TV your victim has, and enter the code in the remote. Then sneak up outside their window while they're watching TV. Start randomly changing channels. When they try to adjust their remote, change the channel again...and again...

STUCK ON YOU

Leave a special message for that special person on their lawn—with plastic forks. Just stick them into the ground to spell out your personal note.

TOP 10 PRACTICAL JOKES, PART 2

Ready for more? Remember: These are for informational purposes only. Uncle John accepts no responsibility if you choose to actually try one of these pranks.

4. What the...?

Keep a copy of yesterday's paper. Then before anyone in your family gets to read today's paper, replace the middle section with yesterday's. Then laugh yourself silly when your dad can't find the rest of the cover story!

5. Everyone's a Winner

Next time your mom or dad gets money from an ATM, scream at the top of your lungs, "We won! We won! This is the third time this week!"

6. Zoo Panic

Put the cap on a great day at the zoo with this prank. Just as you exit the zoo, run toward the parking lot, yelling, "Run for your lives, they're loose!"

7. Cuppah Showah

Fill a plastic cup with water, then set it on an upper shelf of a kitchen or bathroom cabinet. Take a short length of thread and tape one end to the cup and the other to the inside of the cabinet door. The next person to open the cabinet gets a shower!

For Part 3, turn to page 229.

Silly Songs & Rhymes

MOUSE TALES

Hickory dickory dock!

The mice ran up the clock.

The clock struck one...

And the other mouse escaped with only minor injuries.

NUTTY NURSERY RHYMES

SOMETHING ABOUT MARY

1. Mary had a little lamb...
The doctor had a cow.

2. Mary had a
swarm of bees,
And they, to save their lives,
Went everywhere that Mary went
'cause Mary had the hives.

3. Mary had a little lamb.
She fed it castor oil.
Everywhere
that Mary went,
It fertilized
the soil.

KNOCK KNOCK JOKES

Knock-knock!
Who's there?
Adolf.
Adolf who?
Adolf ball hit me in de mowf. Dat's why I dawk dis way.

Knock-knock!
Who's there?
Andy.
Andy who?
Andy green grass grows all around, all around, Andy green grass grows all around.

Animal Jokes

Some race horses are having a conversation. One of them starts to boast about his track record. "In the last 15 races, I've won 8 of them!"

Another horse breaks in, "Well, in the last 27 races, I've won 19!"

"Oh, that's good, but in the last 36 races, I've won 28!" says another, flicking his tail.

At this point, they notice that a Greyhound dog has been sitting there, listening. "I don't mean to boast," says the Greyhound, "but in my last 90 races, I've won 88 of them!"

The horses are clearly amazed. "Wow!" says one, after a hushed silence. "A talking dog!"

Why do gorillas
have big nostrils?
Because they
have big fingers!

WHY DON'T
RHINOS SMOKE?
BECAUSE THEIR BUTTS
ARE TOO BIG TO FIT
IN THE ASHTRAY.

WHAT DO YOU
CALL THE BAD
LION TAMER?
CLAUDE
BOTTOM!

Why didn't the
hippopotamus
pick his nose?
He didn't know
where to hide a
30-pound booger.

WHAT DO YOU
GET IF YOU POUR
BOILING WATER
DOWN A RABBIT
HOLE?
HOT CROSS
BUNNIES.

What do you
call it when a
lawnmower runs
over a bird's nest?
Shredded tweet.

GAMES

SILLY FUN

Bored? Go have fun with some of these suggestions from Uncle John, the Funmeister.

1. Have a picnic in an elevator, complete with checkered tablecloth and sliced watermelon! Invite elevator riders to join you.

2. Go ice blocking! Get several blocks of ice from the grocery store, grab some friends, and ride the ice blocks down a long grassy hill. No hills where you live? Have ice-block relay races. These are just like a wheelbarrow race: one kid sits on the ice while the other kid pushes. Then switch. (Be prepared for frozen butts.)

Riddles & More Riddles

A bus with no passengers stops, and five people get on. At the next stop eight people get on. At the next stop six people get off. How many people are on the bus?

Eight (7 passengers and 1 bus driver.)

How many birthdays does the average kid have?

One.

A man lives in a house with four walls. Each wall has a window. Each window faces south. A bear walks by. What color is the bear?

The only place each window could face south is at the North Pole. So the bear must have been a polar bear. White.

BE A CHEESE WHIZ

Make cheese in your own kitchen. Here's how:

What You Need

- 1 quart milk
- Cup
- Medium saucepan
- Wooden spoon
- Colander
- 2 tablespoons lemon juice
- Piece of cheesecloth or a lightweight dishtowel
- Medium bowl

Preparation

1. Pour the 2 tablespoons of lemon juice in the cup.

2. Pour the milk into the saucepan and place on the stove, on medium-high.

3. Stir slowly with the wooden spoon.

4. When bubbles form and the milk begins to boil, remove pan from stove and stir in the lemon juice.

5. Put pan with lemon-milk mixture back on the stove and continue stirring until lumps begin to form.

6. When lumps have formed, turn off the stove and remove saucepan from the burner. Cool for 5 minutes.

7. Put the cheesecloth (or dishtowel) in the colander in the sink. Pour cooled mixture into the colander. The milk will drain through, but the cheese curds will stay.

8. Put the curds in the bowl and put it in the refrigerator to chill.

9. After it's chilled, add a little salt and chow down!

YOU NAME IT

REAL FUNNY NAMES

These are real names of real people. The next time you're bored, pick up a phone book and see what other silly names you can find.

Ura Hogg

Ima Hogg

Crystal Punch

Tripp March

Raken Leaves

June Bugger

Constance Noring

Kill Lawrence

Justin Case

Clark Barr

Marshall Deputy

Joe King

Laurel Hardy

Duc Dung

Harry Scarey

Moon Howling

Rainey Bowels

Merry Christmas

Fern Leaf

Georgia Ham

Duane Plants

Rudolph Christmas

Robin Birdfeather

Pinky Cutter

Fannie Sweat

Jack Rabbit

Moe D. Grass

Leif Booger

Happy Smily

Cislyn Crisp

Stan Dupp

Tom Morrow

Paige Turner

Crushing Blow

Buck Chew

Mei Noodle

B-R-R-R-I-N-G

ANOTHER FUNNY ANSWERING MACHINE MESSAGE

(said very fast)

Hi, we're not home right now. If you want to leave a message, please wait for the tone. If you want to leave your name and number, please press pound, press 3, then dial your name, then press 6 and dial your number. If you want to leave your name and just a message, press star, press 6, ask for extension 4443, then leave your name and message. If you want to leave your number and the time you called, please press star twice, spin in a circle, press 1 twice, talk loud and...BEEEEP!

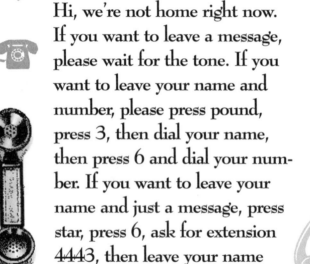

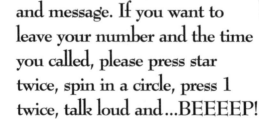

1 Minute Mystery

CRUMPET CRACKS THE CASE

On Sunday morning a man was murdered in his house. His wife called the police. When Detective Crumpet arrived, he asked the wife and each member of the household staff to tell him what they were doing at the time of the murder:

- The wife said she was sleeping.

- The cook was cooking breakfast.

- The maid was getting the mail.

- The gardener was picking vegetables.

- The butler was cleaning the closet.

"Aha!" Crumpet cried. "You're under arrest!" And he clamped a pair of handcuffs on the murderer.

Who was it, and how did the detective know?

You'll find the answer on the next page.

Solution

CRUMPET CRACKS THE CASE

Answer to the puzzle on the previous page:

Whodunit? It was the maid. She said she was getting the mail…but there is no mail on Sunday.

Silly Science

HOW TO LAUNCH A TENNIS BALL

This trick demonstrates the physics of a simple transfer of energy between objects of different masses. It also makes you want to say, "Wow!"

What You Need
- Launch pad (a hard surface like a driveway)
- Basketball
- Tennis ball

How to Launch
1. Stack the tennis ball on top of the basketball.
2. Drop them both at the same time.
3. Step back *fast*!

What Happens
Blastoff! The tennis ball will shoot straight up into the air, and the basketball will stop dead on the launch pad.

How It Works
When you drop the balls together, they pull apart. The bottom one hits the ground first and rebounds into the top ball, which is still on its way down. The result is a head-on collision between balls that have a very different *mass* (the amount of matter in an object). Much of the energy of the first ball gets transferred to the second ball, which sends it soaring up, up, and away!

Variation: If you want to see a ball *really* fly, load a Ping-Pong ball on top of a large super ball (about the size of a tennis ball)—and drop 'em!

A man takes his Rottweiler to the vet and says, "My dog's cross-eyed. Is there anything you can do for him?"

"Well, let's have a look at him."

The vet picks up the dog and examines his eyes, then checks his teeth.

Finally, he says, "I'm going to have to put him down."

"Why? Because he's cross-eyed?"

"No, because he's really heavy."

KNOCK KNOCK JOKES

Knock-knock!
Who's there?
Ach.
Ach who?
Gesundheit!

Knock-knock!
Who's there?
Andrew.
Andrew who?
Ann-drew on the wall and *boy*, is she in trouble!

KNOCK-KNOCK!

WHO'S THERE?

TOM SAWYER

TOM SAWYER WHO?

TOM SAWYER UNDERWEAR.

Knock-knock!
Who's there?
Dishes.
Dishes who?
Dishes me.
Whoish you?

Knock-knock!
Who's there?
Hans.
Hans who?
Hans up, this is a robbery.

A blind man was walking down the street with his seeing-eye dog one day. They came to a busy intersection, and the dog, ignoring the steady stream of cars zooming by, led the blind man right out into the thick of traffic. Tires screeched and horns blared as panicked drivers tried desperately not to run the pair down.

The blind man and the dog finally reached the safety of the sidewalk on the other side of the street. The blind man pulled a cookie out of his coat pocket and offered it to the dog.

A passerby, having observed the near-fatal incident, couldn't control his amazement and said to the blind man, "Why on Earth are you rewarding your dog with a cookie? He nearly got you killed!"

The blind man replied, "For your information, I'm trying to find out which end his head is, so I can kick his butt!"

The class assignment was to write about something unusual that happened during the past week.

When little Irving got up to read, he began by saying, "Dad fell in the well last week..."

"Good heavens," shrieked his teacher. "Is he all right now?"

"He must be," said little Irving. "He stopped yelling for help yesterday."

Two muffins are baking in the oven. One muffin turns to the other muffin and says, "Boy, it sure is hot in here." The other muffin screams, "*Aaah!* A talking muffin!"

GOOD SPORTS

A little boy was talking to himself as he strutted through the backyard, wearing his baseball cap and toting a ball and bat. "I'm the greatest hitter in the world," he said.

Then he tossed the ball into the air, swung at it, and missed.

"Strike one!" he announced.

He picked up the ball and said again, "I'm the greatest hitter in the world!" Again he tossed the ball into the air, swung...and missed.

"Strike two!"

The boy took a moment to look at his bat and ball carefully. He spit on his hands and rubbed them together. He straightened his cap and said once more, "I'm the greatest hitter in the world!"

Once again he tossed the ball up in the air and swung at it. He missed.

"Strike three!"

Then he said, "Wow! I'm the greatest *pitcher* in the world!"

The Three Little Pigs went to dinner one night, and the waiter asked them what they'd like to drink.

"I would like a Sprite," said the first little piggy.

"I would like a Coke," said the second little piggy.

"I want water, lots and lots of water," said the third little piggy.

The waiter brought them their drinks and then took their dinner orders.

"I want a nice big steak," said the first piggy.

"I would like the salad plate," said the second piggy.

"I want water, lots and lots of water," said the third little piggy.

The meals were served and after a while, the waiter asked if the piggies would like any dessert.

"I want a banana split," said the first piggy.

"I want a root beer float," said the second piggy.

"I want water, lots and lots of water!" exclaimed the third little piggy.

"Pardon me for asking," the waiter said, "but why have you only ordered water all evening?"

The third piggy said, "Well, somebody has to go wee, wee, wee, all the way home!"

SEEING IS BELIEVING

Or is it? Remember—not everything is as it seems. You'll find the solutions on the next page.

OPTICAL ILLUSION
The challenge: Can you tell which diagonal line on the left matches up with the diagonal line on the right?

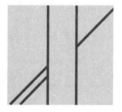

X-TREME TIC-TAC-TOE
The challenge: Can you place six X's on a tic-tac-toe grid without making three in a row in any direction?

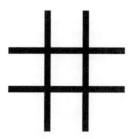

Solutions

SEEING IS BELIEVING

Answers from previous page.

OPTICAL ILLUSION

X-TREME TIC-TAC-TOE

"Doctor! Doctor! I think I've turned into a dog!"

"Sit down on this chair and tell me about it."

"I can't, I'm not allowed on the furniture."

"DOCTOR! DOCTOR! EVERYONE THINKS I'M A LIAR!"

"I JUST CAN'T BELIEVE THAT."

"Doctor! Doctor! I keep seeing funny spots before my eyes!"

"Have you seen a doctor before?"

"No, just funny spots."

"DOCTOR! DOCTOR! WHENEVER I DRINK JUICE I GET A PAIN IN MY EYE!"

"WELL, TRY TAKING THE STRAW OUT OF THE GLASS."

B-R-R-R-i-N-G

MORE ANSWERING MACHINE MESSAGES

(For Shakespeare lovers)

So long as phones can ring
and eyes can see,
Please leave a message,
and I'll get back to thee.

After the tone, leave your name and number and tell me where you hid the money.

Hello. I'm David's answering machine. What are you?

Hi there. This is Joe speaking. I'm home right now and in a moment, I'll have a decision to make. Leave your name and number and I'll start thinking about it...

MAGIC

7-11-13 TRICK!

*Mystify your friends with the
blazing speed of your brain.*

Issue this challenge to your friend: You can get the
answer to a complicated multiplication problem
before he does, even though he'll be using a calculator.

Have him write down a three-digit number, such as
452 or 993, on a piece of paper and give the paper to
you. You give him a calculator.

Then have him:

1. Enter the three-digit number on the calculator.

2. Multiply the number by 7.

3. Multiply that number by 11.

4. And, finally, multiply his subtotal by 13.

While he's busy calculating, you just write down the
answer on the piece of paper.

THE SECRET: All you do is write out the
starting number twice! So 452 would become
452,452 and 993 would become 993,993.

Jokes

What do you call cheese that isn't yours?

Nacho cheese.

HOW DOES THE MOON CUT HIS HAIR?

E-CLIPSE IT.

What do sea monsters eat?

Fish and ships.

Jokes

Jokes

What do you call the ghost who haunts TV shows?

Phantom of the Oprah.

WHY DON'T BLIND PEOPLE LIKE TO SKYDIVE?

BECAUSE IT SCARES THE seeing-eye DOG.

Jokes

Animal Jokes

What do you call a fish without an eye?
A fsh.

IS IT HARD TO SPOT A LEOPARD?
NO, THEY COME THAT WAY.

What snakes are good at math?
Adders.

Do we get fur from a skunk?
Yes, as fur away as possible.

During a recent downpour a man observed, "It's raining cats and dogs today."

"Don't I know it," observed his friend. "I just stepped in a poodle."

What do you get when you cross a cow and a duck?
Milk and quackers!

What kind of hat does Sir Lancelot wear?

A knight cap.

Leonardo DiCaprio, Tom Hanks, and Arnold Schwarzenegger were making a movie about famous composers.

Leo said, "I'll be Beethoven." Tom said, "I'll be Tchaikovsky." Arnold said, "I'll be Bach!"

What do you get if you divide the circumference of your jack-o'-lantern by its diameter?

Pumpkin pi.

WHO GOES FiRST?

Can you solve this puzzle?
(Answer on next page.)

Brain Teasers

A man went on a trip with a fox, a goose, and a sack of corn.

He came to a river and found the only way across was in a little boat. But the boat was too small to hold them all. He could ferry them over one at a time...

...but he couldn't leave the fox alone with the goose, or the goose alone with the corn.

How did he get them all safely across the river?

Solution

Answers for the previous page.

WHO GOES FIRST?

The man took the goose over the river first and came back. Then he took the fox over and brought the goose back. Next he took the corn over and came back alone to get the goose. Finally he took the goose over, picked up the fox and the sack of corn, and went on his way.

Monster Jokes

Why couldn't Dracula's wife get to sleep?

Because of his coffin.

Why wasn't there any food left after the monster party?

Because everyone was a goblin.

WHAT MONSTER FLIES HIS KITE IN A RAINSTORM?

BENJAMIN FRANKLINSTEIN.

WHAT KIND OF MISTAKES DO SPOOKS MAKE? *BOO-BOOS.*

"Mommy, mommy, I'm going to be sick," a little girl whispered in church.

"Run outside to the bushes next to the church," her mother told her.

Five minutes later, the little girl returned.

"Did you throw up?" her mother asked.

"Yes," said the little girl, "but I didn't have to go all the way to the bushes. There was a box near the front door that said, 'For the Sick.'"

Jokes & Puns

Ho Ho!

Tee Hee...

yuk!

Ho Ho!

Tee Hee...

TEACHER: What is the chemical formula for water?

PAUL: HIJKLMNO.

Ho Ho!

TEACHER: What are you talking about?

Tee Hee...

Yuk!

PAUL: Yesterday you told us it was H to O!

Yuk!

Yuk!

HA!

Tee Hee...

chortle...

HA!

Tee Hee...

chortle...

Ho Ho!

Tee Hee...

Yuk!

chortle...

Yuk!

HA!

An American was knocked uncon-scious in a traffic accident in Australia. The ambulance rushed him to a local hospital. When he woke up hours later, he asked the doctor, "What happened? Was I brought here to die?"

YUK!

HA!

Ho Ho!

HO HO!

"No," said the doctor, "you were brought here yester-die."

Ho Ho!

HA!

YUK!

Ha!

HA!

TeeHee...

chortle...

A TRUE STORY

A crook planned to rob the Zions Bank in Salt Lake City. Only problem: he arrived too early—the bank wasn't open yet. So what did he do? He stood outside, waiting in line with the bank's customers. But since he was wearing a face mask and hooded sweater, security guards got suspicious and called the police...who arrested him.

PULL
MY
FINGER

What button won't you
find in a tailor's shop?

A belly button.

Were you long in
the hospital?

*No, I was the same
size that I am now.*

WHY DO FARTS STINK?

*SO DEAF PEOPLE CAN
ENJOY THEM TOO.*

ELEPHANT JOKES

What do you do with a blue elephant?

Cheer him up.

Why did the Frenchman sprinkle salt on the road?

To keep elephants away.

But there are no elephants in France.

See? It's working!

Where is the best place to see a herd of charging elephants?

On elevision.

WHAT IS BIG AND GRAY AND MUTTERS?

A MUMBO JUMBO.

How do you keep an elephant from charging?

Take away his credit card.

How do you make an elephant float?

With two scoops of ice cream, a bottle of root beer, and an elephant.

A GROANER

A frog walked into a bank to see the loan officer, Miss Patricia Wack. He said "Hi! My name is Kermit Jagger. I'm Mick Jagger's son, and I need a loan."

So Miss Wack said, "What do you have that we can hold until you pay us back?" Kermit pulled out a pink ceramic elephant.

So Miss Wack walked into her boss's office and said, "There is a frog out here named Kermit Jagger and he wants a loan. All he has for collateral is a pink ceramic elephant. What the heck is this thing anyway?"

Her boss replied "It's a knick-knack, Patty Wack, give the frog a loan. His old man's a Rolling Stone."

(GROOOOOAN!)

Graffiti

Very funny, Scotty, now beam down my clothes.

I'M GOING TO LIVE FOREVER... OR DIE TRYING!

Have you ever stopped to think and forgot to start again?

"The trouble with the rat race is that even if you win, you're still a rat."
—Lily Tomlin

How do you draw a blank?

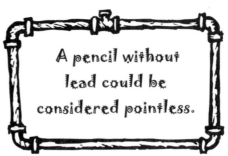

A pencil without lead could be considered pointless.

Old kings never die, they just get throne away.

I'd give my right hand to be ambidextrous.

YOU ARE DEPRIVING SOME POOR VILLAGE OF ITS IDIOT.

YOU'RE GROUNDED

A ROTTEN PRANK

If you play this dirty trick on someone, you'll be spending a lot of quality time alone in your room...

POOL POLLUTION

Want to clear the public pool in a hurry? Buy a Baby Ruth candy bar at the snack bar. Unwrap it and drop in the pool near the lifeguard.

Yell out: "Ew, gross! Somebody pooped in the pool."

Now stand back as everyone leaps out of the water, gagging.

GO TO

JAIL

Teacher: Now class, we know there are 60 seconds in a minute, 60 minutes in an hour, 24 hours in a day, and 365 days in a year. So who can tell me how many seconds there are in a year?

Jason: I know! I know!

Teacher: Yes, Jason, how many seconds are there in a year?

Jason: Twelve!

Teacher: How on Earth did you come up with that number?

Jason: Well, there's January second, February second, March second...

Brain Teasers

Out in Zack's garage there's a barrel with some oil in it.

"This barrel of oil is more than half full," said Zack.

"No it's not," said his helper, Bud. "It's less than half full."

Without using measuring devices or taking any oil from the barrel, how can they prove which one of them is right?

Solution

Answers for previous page.

BARREL-LY FULL

All Zack and Bud have to do is tilt the barrel until the oil just touches the lip of the barrel. If they can see the bottom of the barrel, then the barrel is less than half full and Bud is right. If the bottom of the barrel is still completely covered by the oil, then it is more than half full and Zack is right.

GAMES

HUMAN STRING RELAY

An action-packed game guaranteed to make any party FUN!

What You Need: Two spoons and two balls of yarn.

How to Play: 1. Divide up into two teams. Give each team a ball of yarn with a spoon tied to the end of the yarn. Line up each team single file, facing each other.

2. On "GO!" the first person from each team threads the spoon down his shirt and out his pant leg. When the spoon comes out of his pant leg, he passes it to the next teammate.

3. The leader must still hold onto the ball of yarn, unreeling the yarn as needed while the next player threads the spoon through her shirt and pants.

4. The spoon goes through the entire line and when it reaches the end, it must come back. In reverse! As it does, the leader winds the yarn back into a ball.

5. The first team to finish is the winner!

A SILLY SONG

Lucy Had a Steamboat

Ms. Lucy had a steamboat,
    The steamboat had a bell.
Ms. Lucy went to heaven,
    But the steamboat went to...

Hello, operator,
    Give me number nine,
And if you disconnect me
    I will chop off your...

Behind the 'frigerator
    There was a piece of glass.
Ms. Lucy sat upon it
    And cut her little ...

Ask me no more questions,
    I'll tell you no more lies.
The boys are in the bathroom
    Pulling down their...

Flies are in the meadow,
    The meadow's in the park.
The boys and girls are kissing in the
D.A.R.K, D.A.R.K, D.A.R.K, dark, dark, dark!

SAY IT, DON'T SPRAY IT

*Another tumble of twisters
for the nimble of tongue.*

Three Quick Shots

· She shot three shy thrushes.

· Fran feeds fish fresh
fish food.

· Ike ships ice chips in
ice chip ships.

...and One Long Shot

I'm a sheet slitter.
I slit sheets.
I am the best sheet slitter
that ever slit a sheet.

HOW TO MAKE BIRD POOP

It looks disgusting!
But it tastes great!

What You Need
- Large mixing bowl
- Wooden spoon or spatula
- Large sheet of wax paper
- Medium microwavable bowl

Ingredients
- 5 cups crunchy cereal
- 3 cups crispy rice cereal
- 2-1/2 cups mini marsh-mallows
- 1 bag white chocolate chips
- 2 cups skinny pretzel sticks (break them up if they're long)

Preparation
Mix the dry ingredients in the large bowl. Melt the white chocolate in the microwave for about 1 minute. Pour the melted chocolate over the dry ingredients and spread on wax paper to cool. Once it's cool, break into chunks that look like gross bird poop.

The Prank
With a handful of bird poop you can gross out your friends by eating it off a park bench or a parked car. (Just make sure you're not eating the wrong stuff!)

While sportfishing off the Florida coast, a tourist capsized his boat. He knew how to swim, but his fear of alligators kept him clinging to the overturned craft.

Spotting an old beachcomber standing on the shore, the tourist shouted, "Are there any gators around here?"

"Naw," the man hollered back, "they ain't been around for years!"

Feeling safe, the tourist started swimming leisurely toward shore.

About halfway there he asked the guy, "How'd you get rid of the gators?"

"We didn't do nothin'," the beachcomber said. "The sharks got 'em."

HELLO JELL-O

Here's a fun prank to play on someone who'll still be your friend after you prank them.

Sneak into your target's bathroom and pour a packet of lemon Jell-O into the toilet (make sure to play this prank late at night because the Jell-O needs some time to harden). Then wait for your target to make the morning bathroom run. Imagine their surprise when they see their poop sitting on top of the squiggly Jell-O.

(Don't worry—no harm's been done. Just break up the Jell-O to flush the toilet.)

YOU NAME IT

READ 'EM AND LAUGH!

More silly book titles we'd like to see.

The Worst Journey in the World, by Helen Back

Bird Watching, by I. C. A. Duck

The Story of Sherwood Forest, by Robin D. Rich

Telephone Problems, by Ron Number

Reptiles, by Sally Mander

Jack Be Nimble, by Jack B. Quick

The Winner!, by Vic Torius

How Plants Eat, by Oz Moses

The Stargazer, by C. D. Skye

Disgusting Foods, by Henrietta Moth

How to Find Things, by Luke A. Round

Weekend Breaks, by Gladys Friday

Dogs, by Kay Nine

Winning the Lottery, by Jack Potts

How to Make Money, by Robin Banks

Don't Leave without Me, by Isa Coming

Mashed Carrots, by Bebe Food

Mind over Matter, by Ben D. Spoon

Jokes

HA!

Tee Hee...

Ho Ho!

Tee Hee...

Ho Ho!

Tee Hee...

Yuk!

Ho Ho!

Tee Hee...

What kind of briefs does Thor wear?

Thunderpants.

What do you get when you cross a dog with a soldier?

A pooper trooper.

Yuk!

Yuk!

Yuk!

Tee Hee...

chortle...

HA!

Tee Hee...

chortle...

chortle...

Yuk!

HA!

Ho Ho!

HO HO!

How do you make a Kleenex dance?

Put a little boogie in it.

What is even smarter than a talking bird?

A spelling bee.

Ho Ho!

Yuk!

YUK!

HA!

How do you get two Tarzans in the refrigerator?

You can't. There's only one Tarzan!

Ho Ho!

HA!

YUK!

Ha!

TeeHee...

chortle...

A small boy is sent to bed by his father. Five minutes later: "Da-ad, I'm thirsty. Can I have a drink of water?"

"No. You had your chance. Lights out."

Five minutes later: "Da-aaaad..."

"WHAT?!?"

"I'm THIRSTY. Can I have a drink of water?"

"I told you NO! If you ask again I'll have to spank you!"

"Five minutes later: "Daaa-aaad..."

"WHAT?!"

"When you come in to spank me, can you bring me a drink of water?"

Silly Science

HOW TO BEND WATER

Think it can't be done? Think again.

What You Need
1 nylon comb
1 water faucet

Preparation

Turn on the faucet to make a thin stream of water. Run the comb through your hair several times. Slowly bring the teeth of the comb near the stream of water, about 3 or 4 inches below the faucet. When the teeth of the comb are about an inch or less away from the falling water, it will bend toward the comb.

How It Works

The secret is *static electricity*, which is the accumulation of an electrical charge in an object. That charge is created when two objects are rubbed against each other. Hair and nylon are particularly good at building up a charge when they are rubbed together. The electrical charge you built up on the comb by running it through your hair attracts the molecules in the stream of water, so it bends toward the comb.

SEEiNG iS BELiEViNG

Or is it? Remember—not everything is as it seems. You'll find the solutions on the next page.

FIVE PLUS SIX = NINE?

The challenge: Can you add five toothpicks to these six and make nine?

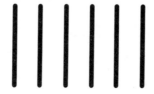

A PIECE OF PIE

The challenge: With just 12 toothpicks, can you make six identical triangles?

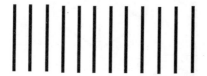

Solutions

SEEING IS BELIEVING

Answers for the previous page.

FIVE PLUS SIX = NINE?

NINE

A PIECE OF PIE

LOOK SMART!

Impress your friends with these weird facts.

- Peanuts are one of the ingredients in dynamite.
- You burn more calories sleeping than watching TV.

- In March 1989, a solar storm knocked out electrical power in eastern Canada for nine hours and caused garage doors in San Francisco to open and shut as if by magic.

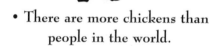

- There are more chickens than people in the world.
- There's a reference to Superman in every episode of *Seinfeld*.
- You can't lick your elbow.
- A snail can sleep for three years.
- It is physically impossible for pigs to look up into the sky.

MAGIC

COIN OF MYSTERY

Demonstrate the powers of mind over matter when you balance a quarter on your fingertips.

What You Need: 1 quarter and 1 straight pin

The Setup

Hide the pin between the first two fingers of one hand (do this before you start the trick). With the other hand, take a quarter out of your pocket. Let the audience inspect it to make sure you haven't tampered with it.

The Trick

Lay the coin down on top of the pin in your other hand. Raise the coin to a standing position near the ends of your fingers. Raise the pin with it, but make sure no one sees it. Keep pressure on the pin held between your two fingers, and the quarter will balance on your finger as if by magic. Then slowly release pressure on the pin and the coin will drift down onto your fingers. While you let your audience look at the coin again, put the pin in your pocket.

Why do bagpipers walk when they play?

They're trying to get away from the noise.

WHY DID THE ATOM CROSS THE ROAD?

IT WAS TIME TO SPLIT.

WHAT KIND OF ILLNESS DOES JACKIE CHAN GET?

KUNG FLU.

Why did the Pilgrims' pants always fall down?

Because they wore their belt buckles on their hats.

MATH-MAGICAL

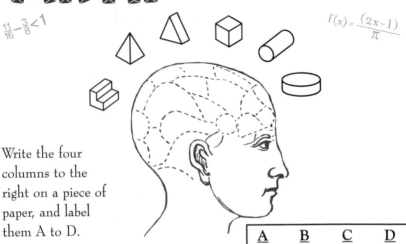

$\frac{11}{16} - \frac{3}{8} < 1$

$f(x) = \frac{(2x-1)}{\pi}$

Write the four columns to the right on a piece of paper, and label them A to D.

Give the piece of paper to a friend and ask her to think of a number between 1 and 15. Now ask her to tell you which of the columns that number appears in. Without even looking at the list of numbers, you tell her the number she had in mind!

A	B	C	D
1	2	4	8
7	6	13	10
5	3	15	14
3	15	7	13
11	7	6	15
9	10	5	12
13	14	12	11
15	11	14	9

How It Works

Memorize the top four numbers: 1, 2, 4, 8. When your friend tells you which columns her number is in, add the top numbers from those columns *only* and you'll have her number!

EXAMPLE

Your friend says her number is in column A, C, and D. Add together the top numbers in each of these columns (1 + 4 + 8) to come up with the secret number: 13.

TOP 10 PRACTICAL JOKES, PART 3

Uncle John will not, does not, and cannot, in good conscience, recommend that you actually try one of these pranks...but if you do, wear sneakers. (To help you make a fast getaway.)

8. Numb Butts

Bring a tube of sports ointment (such as Ben-Gay or Icy Hot) to school and smear it all over the toilet seats in the restrooms. See how many students and teachers have to suffer with numb butts before they figure out what's happened.

9. Rude Awakening

Wait until your victim is asleep. Then sneak up on them in the dark. Aim a flashlight at their closed eyes. As you flick it on, yell, "Train!" *(NEVER do this trick to anyone with a heart condition!)*

10. Snap-Pop Potty

Place several party snaps (those little snap-pops that make a "bang" when you throw them on the ground) under a toilet seat, then gently lower it the rest of the way. When your victim sits down on the throne:

KERPOW!

Monster Jokes

WHY DOESN'T DRACULA HAVE ANY FRIENDS?

BECAUSE HE'S A PAIN IN THE NECK.

Why don't witches like to ride their brooms when they're angry?

They're afraid of flying off the handle!

Who did Frankenstein take to the prom?

His ghoul friend.

Why did the monster eat a lightbulb?

He only wanted a light snack.

One cold winter day an old man walked out onto a frozen lake, cut a hole in the ice, and dropped in his fishing line. He'd been sitting there for an hour without a nibble when a young boy walked out onto the ice. He cut a hole in the ice not too far from the old man and dropped in his fishing line. A minute later, *wham!* a huge bass bit the kid's hook and the boy pulled in the fish. The old man couldn't believe it, but figured it was just luck. But the boy dropped in his line again and a few minutes later pulled in another one.

This went on and on until finally the old man couldn't stand it anymore. "Son, I've been out here for over an hour without even a nibble," he said. "You've been here only a few minutes and have caught about half a dozen fish! How do you do it?"

The boy smiled and said, "Roo raf roo reep ra rums rarm."

"What was that?" the old man asked.

Again the boy said, "Roo raf roo reep ra rums rarm."

"Look," said the old man, "I can't understand a word you are saying."

So the boy spit into his hand and said, "You have to keep the worms warm!"

Jokes & Puns !

Tee Hee... Ho Ho! HA! yuk! Ho Ho!

What do you get when you
follow an earthquake with a fire?
Shake and bake.

**Why was the bride sad on
her wedding day?**
**She doesn't get to marry
the best man.**

HA! Tee Hee... chortle... HA! Tee Hee... chortle... Ho Ho!

Tee Hee...

Did you hear about the canary who fell
into a can of varnish and drowned?

*It was a sad way to die, but
he had a beautiful finish.*

A woman rushed out to
the garbage truck in an old
raggedy robe and her hair in
curlers. "Am I too late for
the garbage?" she cried.

"No," the driver
replied. "Hop in!"

Yuk! Yuk! Yuk! chortle... Yuk! HA! Ho Ho! HO HO! Yuk! YUK! HA! Ho Ho! HA! YUK! Ha!

TeeHee... chortle...

A father noticed that his son was spending way too much time playing computer games and not doing his homework.

"When Abe Lincoln was your age," the dad lectured, "he was studying books by the light of the fireplace."

"Oh yeah?" replied the son. "When Lincoln was *your* age, he was president of the United States."

Artsy-Fartsy
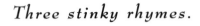

Three stinky rhymes.

F is for Fart.
It stirs up a breeze.
And smells even worse
than Limburger cheese.

There was a young fellow from Cager

Who, as a result of a wager,
Offered to fart
The whole oboe part
Of Mozart's Quartet in F Major.

Here I Sit

Here I sit all brokenhearted,
Had to poop but only farted.
Yesterday I took a chance,
Tried to fart but pooped my pants.

* * *

Q: What's the definition of a surprise?
A: A fart with a lump in it.

Recipes

Wanna really gross people out? Try whipping up your own fake doggie doo!

What You Need

- A pastry cone. (You can find these at the grocery store in the cake decorating section.)
- 1/4 cup chunky-looking foods (like raisins and lumpy oatmeal)
- 1 can dog food
- 1/2 cup bean dip

Preparation

Mix the whole mess together in a mixing bowl until it looks like a big bowl of poop. Now load it into the caulking tube.

Pranking with "Le Poop du Jour"

Go to the nearest park and squeeze out a gigantic pile onto the grass or sidewalk. Then wait for the next dog walker to stroll by. The walker will be totally grossed out when their dog gobbles up the poop treat!

Insults

YO' BROTHER IS SO STUPID...

- ...he tried to steal a free sample.
- ...he put a ruler in his bed to see how long he slept.
- ...he thought a "quarterback" was a refund.
- ...he went to the Gap to get his teeth fixed.
- ...he sat on the TV and watched the couch.
- ...he threw a rock at the ground and missed.

- ...I told him Christmas was just around the corner and he went looking for it.

- ...he thought a lawsuit was something you wear to court.

YO' SISTER IS SO UGLY...

- ...she looked in a mirror and her reflection ran away.
- ...her mother used to feed her with a slingshot.
- ...she turned Medusa to stone.
- ...she made an onion cry.
- ...when she got in the tub, the water jumped out.
- ...her pillow cries at night.
- ...her shadow quit.

- ...when she joined an ugly contest, they said, "Sorry, no professionals."

- ...she didn't get hit with the ugly stick, she got hit with the whole tree!

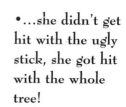

Gross Songs

How dry I am,
How wet I'll be,
If I don't find
The bathroom key.

I found the key,
I lost the door,
I'll have to do
It on the floor.

KNOCK KNOCK JOKES

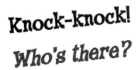

Knock-knock!
Who's there?
Radio.
Radio who?
Radio not,
here I
come.

Knock-knock!
Who's there?
Annie.
Annie who?
Annie body
home?

CHICKEN RIDDLES

Why did the chicken cross the road?
To boldly go where no chicken has gone before!

Why did it take so long for the elephant to cross the road?
Because the chicken had trouble carrying him.

On which side does a chicken have the most feathers?
The outside.

Why did the chicken get in trouble?
Because it used fowl language.

How do you keep a dog from crossing the road?
You put him in a barking lot.

What do you call a chicken crossing the road?
Poultry in motion.

Why did the chicken cross the playground?
To get to the other slide.

Why did the chicken cross the Internet?
To get to the other site.

What do you call a chicken that crosses the road without looking both ways?
   Dead.

Why did the hen go halfway across the road and stop?
She wanted to lay it on the line.

Why did the Roman chicken cross the road?
She was afraid someone would Caesar.

Why did the turkey cross the road?
It was the chicken's day off.

Jokes

Ho Ho !

Tee Hee...

yuk !

Tee Hee...

Ho Ho !

Tee Hee...

Yuk !

Yuk !

Yuk !

HA !

Two trucks loaded with thousands of copies of *Roget's Thesaurus* collided as they left a New York publishing house. According to a newspaper report, witnesses were stunned, startled, flabbergasted, taken aback, stupefied...

Tee Hee...

Ho Ho !

chortle...

chortle...

Ho Ho !

HA !

YUK !

Ha !

A man went to a restaurant and ordered a steak with a baked potato. About halfway through dinner, he called the waitress over and said, "Ma'am, this potato is bad."

She nodded, picked up the potato, and smacked it.

Then she put it back on his plate and said, "Sir, if that potato causes any more trouble, you just let me know."

Ho Ho !

Yuk !

YUK !

HA !

Yuk !

HA !

Ho Ho !

HO HO !

HA!

Tee Hee...

chortle...

TWISTED CHRISTMAS CAROLS

JINGLE BELLS

Jingle Bells, Santa smells,
Rudolph pulled the sleigh;
Stuffed his nose with Cheerios,
And ate them all the way—hey!

WE THREE KINGS

We three kings of Orient are
Smoking on a lighted cigar.
It was loaded,
It exploded—blam!—Silent Night.

LET IT SNOW!

(as sung by Captain Jean-Luc Picard
of the Starship Enterprise)

Oh, the vacuum outside is endless,
Unforgiving, cold, and friendless,
But still we must boldly go—
Make it so, make it so, make it so!

HEY, WHO'S THE FAT GUY IN THE RED SUIT?

One year, Santa and his reindeer landed on an outdoor toilet.

Santa hollered out, "I SAID, THE *SCHMIDT* HOUSE!"

WHAT DO YOU CALL SANTA'S HELPERS? SUBORDINATE CLAUSES.

Why does Santa Claus go down the chimney on Christmas Eve?

Because it soots him.

What goes "Ho ho plop"? Santa Claus laughing his head off.

YOU NAME IT

STRANGE TOWN NAMES

INK, ARKANSAS

When a local school teacher sent out notes asking people to vote for a town name, she was afraid their replies would be illegible. So she told them to "write in ink." Which they did, literally spelling it out—and Ink got the most votes.

SCRATCH ANKLE, ALABAMA

Folks passing by noticed that scratching mosquito bites seemed to be the only thing residents of this town did as they sat on their porches in the summer.

PECULIAR, MISSOURI

Three times the name selected by locals was turned down because it was already used by another town. So they were told to pick a name that was "peculiar," so they did.

GAS, KANSAS

No one knows how the tiny town of Gas got its name, but locals sure love telling anyone who goes by, "Don't blink or you'll pass Gas!"

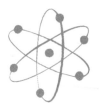

Silly Science

COLLAPSE THE CAN

The air around us is a powerful force of nature, as this trick demonstrates. (Note: You will need a grownup to help you with this.)

What You Need

- Empty aluminum soft-drink can
- 2- or 3-quart saucepan
- A pair of kitchen tongs
- Tablespoon

Preparation

Fill the pan with cold water and set on the kitchen counter. Put 1 tablespoon of water in the empty can. Heat the can on the stove until steam comes out of the opening. Let it cook 30 more seconds. Turn off the stove. Use the tongs to grasp the can. Turn it upside down and dip it into the cold water in the pan. FWOOMP! The can will collapse.

How It Works

Heating the can makes the water inside it boil. The steam from the boiling water pushes all the air out of the can. Once the can is full of steam, you cool it suddenly by turning it over and dipping it in the cold water. Cooling the can makes the steam condense, leaving the can empty. When the can is empty, the pressure of the air outside crushes it.

CAUTION: Don't heat the can over high heat or heat it when it's empty. If you do, the ink may burn or the aluminum might melt.

UPSIDE-DOWN GLASS OF WATER

Warning: Always do this experiment over a sink to make sure the floor doesn't get soaked.

What You Need

· 1 small drinking glass.

· 1 playing card from a deck of cards (make sure it's one you don't need anymore, because it will get wet!)

Preparation

Fill the drinking glass half way with water. Place the card over the top of the drinking glass. Make sure the card covers the mouth of the glass completely. Put pressure on the card with your hand and carefully turn the glass over. Once the glass is completely upside down, take your hand away from the card. Ta da! The card will stick to the mouth of the glass and the water will stay inside the glass.

How It Works

Two words: air pressure. The air around the glass pushes up against the card harder than the water inside the glass pushes down. In fact, you would need a glass of water almost 30 feet high before the water would weigh enough to push the card off the glass.

B-R-R-R-I-N-G

FUNNY ANSWERING MACHINE MESSAGES

Hello. You're talking to a machine. My owners do not need siding, windows, or a hot tub. They give to charity through the office, they don't need their carpets cleaned or their pictures taken. If you're still with me, leave your name and number and they'll get back to you.

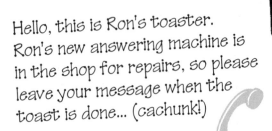

Hello, this is Ron's toaster. Ron's new answering machine is in the shop for repairs, so please leave your message when the toast is done... (cachunk!)

Thank you for calling. If you wish to speak to Tim, push 1 now. If you wish to speak to Lynn, push 2 now. If you have a wrong number, push 3 now. All this button pushing doesn't do anything, but it's a good way to work off frustration and it makes us feel like we have a big-time phone system.

Those little plastic things on the end of your shoelaces are called *aglets*.

GOOD NEWS! CHOCOLATE DOES NOT CAUSE ACNE.

DID YOU KNOW?

A *wobbegong* is an Australian shark.

ANCIENT ROMANS MADE TOOTHPASTE WITH BLOOD, CHARCOAL, HONEY, OIL, AND...GROUND-UP CRAB EYES.

Fish have growth rings just like trees. Just look at their scales. Each ring is called a *circuli*. Clusters of circuli are called *annuli*. One annulus equals one year.

Teacher: "Give me a sentence using the word *gladiator*."

Student: "The lion ate my bossy Aunt Mimi, and I'm glad he ate her!"

"A train smashed into my bicycle, and I didn't even get hurt."

"Why not?"

"My brother Sam was riding it."

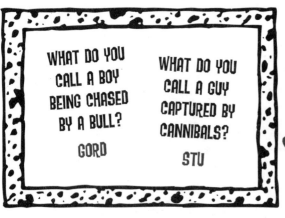

WHAT DO YOU CALL A BOY BEING CHASED BY A BULL?

GORD

WHAT DO YOU CALL A GUY CAPTURED BY CANNIBALS?

STU

Insults

Here are comebacks and wisecracks
for every occasion. Use as needed.

· I'd explain it to you but your brain would explode.

· His breath is so bad, we look forward to his farts!

· She's one Froot Loop shy of a full bowl.

· He hasn't an enemy in the world,
but all his friends hate him.

· Are you a
basketball
player?
No.
Then why are
you dribbling?

· Are you going
to the movies?
No.
Then why are
you picking
your seat?

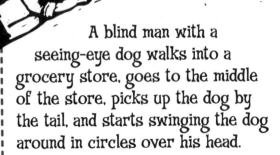

A blind man with a seeing-eye dog walks into a grocery store, goes to the middle of the store, picks up the dog by the tail, and starts swinging the dog around in circles over his head.

The store manager thinks this is quite strange, so he decides to find out what's going on. He approaches the blind man swinging the dog and says, "Pardon me. May I help you with something?"

The blind man says, "No thanks. I'm just looking around."

A LOGIC PUZZLE

Weighty Matter

You have eight marbles. They all look alike, but one is actually heavier than the others. You have a weighing scale with two pans, but you can only use it twice. How can you find out which marble is the heavy one?

You'll find the answer on the next page.

Solution

WEIGHTY MATTER

Answers for the previous page.

Place three marbles on each pan.

- If they balance, remove the marbles from the pans and place the two remaining unweighed marbles on the pans, one on each pan. It will be obvious which is the heavier marble.

- If your first weighing *doesn't* balance, remove the marbles from the lighter pan and place one marble on each pan from the heavier pan. If one side goes down, that's the heavier marble. But if they balance, then the third marble (unweighed) from the heavy pan is the heavy one.

DID YOU KNOW?

Cat urine glows under a black light!

Ancient Egyptians used crushed ant eggs for makeup.

If everyone in the world held hands, the chain would encircle Earth at least 250 times.

FLYING FISH GLIDE ON WIND CURRENTS AS HIGH AS 20 FEET ABOVE THE SURFACE OF THE WATER.

The Brazilian railroad worm produces its own light through a biochemical process called *bioluminescence*. It has a red light on its head and green lights down its side.

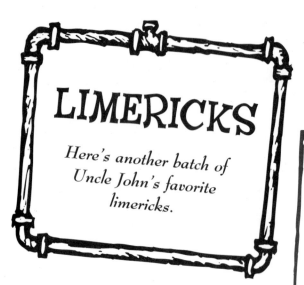

LIMERICKS

Here's another batch of Uncle John's favorite limericks.

A canner, exceedingly canny,
One morning remarked to his granny,
"A canner can can
Anything that he can;
But a canner can't can a can, can he?"

There once was a lady named Sue
Who had nothing whatever to do,
But she did it so badly
I thought she would gladly
Have stopped well before she was through.

SAID A SALTY OLD SKIPPER FROM WALES,
"NUMBER ONE, IT'S ALL RIGHT TO CHEW NAILS.
IT IMPRESSES THE CREW.
(IT IMPRESSES ME, TOO.)
BUT STOP SPITTING HOLES IN THE SAILS!"

GAMES

OPEN SESAME!

A classic card trick.

The Setup

Deal out three stacks of seven cards, face down. Ask a
friend to choose a stack. Pick up the stack he selects
and display the cards in a fan (have the cards facing
out so you can't see them). Then ask your friend
to pick a card, without telling you what it is.

The Trick

1. Put your friend's stack, face down, between the
other two stacks, making one stack of 21 cards.

2. Deal out the cards one at a time into three
stacks of seven, going from left to right.

3. Pick up each stack and show the cards to your
friend. Ask him to say which stack has his card.
(Make sure he doesn't tell you what the card is!)

4. Repeat steps 1 to 3.

The Payoff

Repeat step one. Now say the words "Open sesame!"
Pick up the pile of 21 cards and spell O-P-E-N S-E-S-A-M-E,
dealing one card face down on the table for each letter. The
next card you turn up will be the secret card!

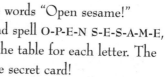

SECRET PHONE CODE

You're in class. You've got to tell your best friend something really important. So you pass her a note. But disaster strikes—the teacher intercepts it! You don't care, though. Why? Because your friend is the only one who can decipher the secret code.

Take a look at your telephone keypad. See the letters under the numbers? By adding strategically placed apostrophes, you can create a terrific secret code! Let's say you want to send the following secret message to your friend:

"Kids rule. Teachers drool."

Here's what it would look like in Secret Phone Code:

5 '4 '3 '7/ 7 8 '5 3// '8 3 '2 2' 4 3 7 7/ '3 7 6' 6' 5'//

How It Works

1. The first word begins with the letter K, which is the middle letter on the 5 button (JKL). So write the number 5 (no apostrophe tells the reader to use the middle letter).

2. The second letter in the first word is I—

it's the last letter on the 4 button (GHI). Write 4'. (The apostrophe *after* the number 4 tells your reader to use the last letter on the 4 button.)

3. The letter D is the first letter on the 3 button (DEF). You write '3. (The apostrophe before the number lets your reader know it's the first letter in its group.)

4. The last letter in the first word is S—it's on the 7 button (PRS). Write S', and end the word with / (forward slash) before you begin another word.

5. Separate each word with a slash. At the end of a sentence, put two slashes.

Looking for a clever way to deliver your message? Slip it into an empty, clean juice box and leave it on your friend's desk. Or cut a slit in a tennis ball, stuff the message inside, and toss it over.

the Graffiti Page

"There's more to life than being really, really, really, really good looking."
—Derek Zoolander

I hate Rachel Prejudice!

"When you sit with a nice girl for two hours, you think it's only a minute. But when you sit on a hot stove for a minute, you think it's two hours. That's relativity."
—Albert Einstein

Learn the rules, then break some.

There are three kinds of people, those who can count and those who can't.

If you can't spell a word, look it up in a dikshunary.

Once I thought I was wrong... but I was mistaken.

GUESSTIMATE

This secret number game will totally surprise everyone! It takes a little bit of work but the results are worth it. All you need is a paper and pencil.

· First multiply the current year by 2 (Example: 2004 x 2 = 4008).

· Next write the answer on a piece of paper. Do NOT let anyone see your secret number!

· Fold the paper and put it in your pocket.

· Now, on another piece of paper, ask a friend to write down the following:

> 1. The year he was born.
> 2. The year he started school.
> 3. How old he'll be at the end of this year.
> 4. How many years he's been in school (at the end of this year).

· Tell your friend to add up all his numbers. Don't let him tell you what they are!

Take out your piece of paper (the one in your pocket) and amaze your friend by showing him your guesstimate— which is the same number he just wrote down!

If you're playing this trick on someone who's already finished high school, have them write down these numbers instead:

> 1. The year they were born.
> 2. The year they graduated from high school.
> 3. How old they will be at the end of this year.
> 4. Number of years since their graduation (at the end of this year).

Once again, their total will equal the number that you secretly wrote down before the trick!

HOW MANY GODS DOES IT TAKE TO CHANGE A LIGHTBULB?

TWO. ONE TO HOLD THE BULB, AND THE OTHER TO ROTATE THE PLANET.

How many actors does it take to change a lightbulb?

Only one— they don't like to share the spotlight.

How many gorillas does it take to change a lightbulb?

Only one, but it sure takes a lot of light bulbs!

How many police officers does it take to screw in a lightbulb?

None. It turned itself in.

Sitting in a tree one day, a robin said to his buddy, "I'm really hungry. Let's fly down and find some lunch."

The birds found a patch of freshly plowed ground that was packed with worms. After they ate, they decided to lie back and bask in the warm sun.

Just then, a big tomcat spied the overstuffed birds. He crept over and gobbled them up.

As the cat washed his face, he purred, "I just love baskin' robins!"

MORE CHICKEN RIDDLES

Q: Why did the chicken end up in the soup?
A: Bad cluck!

Q: What did the chicken do when she saw a bucket of fried chicken?
A: She kicked the bucket!

Q: What do you call a crazy chicken?
A: A cuckoo cluck!

Q: What happened to the chicken whose feathers were all pointing the wrong way?
A: She was tickled to death!

Q: What do chickens grow on?
A: Eggplants!

Q: Why is it easy for chicks to talk?
A: Because talk is cheep!

Q: What do you get when you cross a chicken with a duck?
A: A bird that lays down!

Q: What happens when a hen eats gunpowder?
A: She lays hand gren-eggs!

A LOGIC PUZZLE

SMART CROOK

A thief in ancient times was caught stealing from the king. The usual punishment for the crime was death but the thief begged for mercy. The king decided to be lenient and let the thief choose his own way to die. What way did the thief choose?

Give up? The solutions are on the next page.

Solution

SMART CROOK

Answer for previous page.

The thief chose...
old age.

A new teacher was trying to make use of the psychology courses she'd taken in college. She started her class by saying, "Everyone who thinks they're stupid, stand up!"

After a few seconds, Ronnie stood up. The teacher said, "Do you think you're stupid, Ronnie?"

"No, ma'am, but I hate to see you standing there all by yourself!"

A team of engineers had to measure the height of a flagpole. They only had a measuring tape, and were getting quite frustrated trying to keep the tape along the pole. It kept falling down.

Just then a mathematician came along, saw their problem, and proceeded to remove the pole and lay it on the ground, where he measured it easily.

As he walked away, one engineer said to the other: "Isn't that just like a mathematician? We needed to know the height, and he gave us the length!"

Sharks never stop growing—never! When they lose teeth, they always grow new ones.

THE HUMAN THIGH BONE IS STRONGER THAN CONCRETE.

Americans eat about 350 slices of pizza every second.

DID YOU KNOW?

Hungry cockroaches really will eat your homework. They'll even eat your tennis shoes.

giraffes HAVE BLACK TONGUES.

What do you call
a cat that can
jump really far?

A catapult.

CAT JOKES

What happened when the
cat swallowed a penny?

**There was a little
money in the kitty.**

A veterinarian told a foolish woman that her dog needed some exercise.

"Try playing a game of fetch," the doctor suggested.

"I can't play fetch with my dog," the woman said.

"Why not?" the doctor asked.

"Because he can't throw."

A man walked into a restaurant with his wife. The waiter approached the table and asked for their order.

"I'll have a big steak," the man said. "And make it really rare."

"But sir, what about the mad cow?!" asked the waiter.

"Oh," answered the man, "she'll order for herself."

A duck walks into a drugstore and says, "Gimme some Chapstick and put it on my bill."

What happened after the girl drank eight sodas?

She burped 7-UP.

What's white and lifts weights? An extra-strength aspirin.

Jokes

1st guy: "I just read about a fellow who died after eating six dozen pancakes."

2nd guy: "How waffle."

DAD: "ONLY FOOLS ARE POSITIVE."
SON: "ARE YOU SURE?"
DAD: "I'M POSITIVE."

Jokes

Jokes & Puns !

Tee Hee...
Ho Ho !
Ho Ho !
Yuk !
Tee Hee...
HA !

Two pieces of string meet at a play-ground. One goes on the slide, and the other goes on the swings. They're having a great time until one string decides to go on the merry-go-round.

After a while, the string starts to feel really

dizzy
and
falls
off,

scraping across the asphalt, making a tangled mess of one end, and finally falling in a heap.

The second string looks at him and sighs, "You're not very good on that merry-go-round are you?"

The first string looks at him and says, "I'm a frayed knot."

Yuk !
Yuk !
HA !
Tee Hee
Tee Hee...
chortle...
Yuk !
HA !
Ho Ho !
HO HO !
HA !
Ho Ho !
HA !
YUK !
Ha!

Tee Hee...
HA !
HA !
Tee Hee...
Ho Ho !
Yuk !
YUK !
HA !
chortle...

TeeHee...
chortle...

WORD PUZZLES

Got a minute? See if you can make sense of these wordplays.

1. wear
long

2. r
e
t
t
a
B

3. eggs
easy

4. me snack al

5. pain$S$

6. arrest
you're

7. time time

8. everything
pizza

Answers are on the next page.

Solutions

WORD
PUZZLES

Answers for previous page.

1. Long underwear.

2. Batter up!

3. Eggs over easy.

4. Between-meal snack.

5. Growing pains.

6. You're under arrest.

7. Time after time.

8. Pizza with everything on it.

EPITAPHS

*Some more graveyard humor from
real tombstone inscriptions.*

**In Uniontown,
Pennsylvania:**

Here lies the body
of Jonathan Blake,
Stepped on the gas
Instead of the brake.

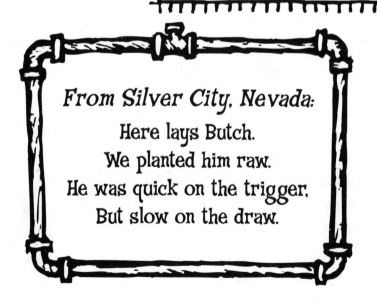

From Silver City, Nevada:

Here lays Butch.
We planted him raw.
He was quick on the trigger,
But slow on the draw.

There was once a snail who was sick and tired of his reputation for being so slow. He decided to get some fast wheels to make up the difference. After shopping around a while, he decided that the Nissan 280Z was the car to get. So the snail goes to the nearest Nissan dealer and says he wants to buy the 280Z, but he wants it repainted "280S".

The dealer asks, "Why 'S'?"

The snail replies, "'S' stands for snail. I want everybody who sees me roaring past to know who's driving."

Well, the dealer doesn't want to lose the unique opportunity to sell a car to a snail, so he agrees to have the car repainted for a small fee.

The snail gets his new car and spent the rest of his days roaring happily down the highway at top speed. And whenever anyone would see him zooming by, they'd say "Wow! Look at that S-car go!"

"So how do they feel?" the sales clerk asked a man trying on a pair of shoes.

"They're a little too tight," the man replied.

"Well, try pulling the tongue out," the clerk suggested.

"Hmmm," the man said. "They thtill thfeel a bith thoo thight."

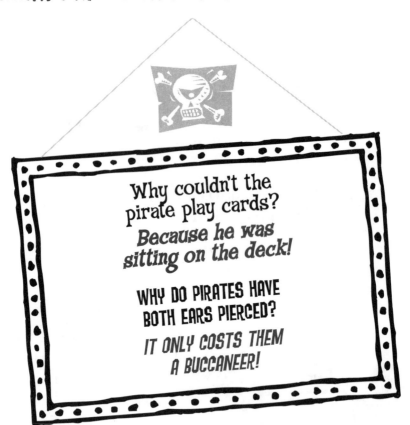

Why couldn't the
pirate play cards?

*Because he was
sitting on the deck!*

WHY DO PIRATES HAVE
BOTH EARS PIERCED?

*IT ONLY COSTS THEM
A BUCCANEER!*

How do mermaids keep in
contact with each other?

They use shell phones.

MATH-MAGICAL

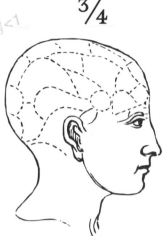

$$\frac{3}{4}$$

$$\frac{1}{4}$$

$$\frac{1}{2}$$

PHONE-Y MATH

Correctly guess someone's phone number, using only a calculator and these cool calculations.

Step 1

Ask your friend to multiply the first 3 digits of their 7-digit phone number by 80 (do not use the area code!) and write the answer on a piece of paper.

Step 2

Now, take the piece of paper and, using your calculator:

• Add 1 to the answer.

• Multiply the new number by 250 and write it down on the piece of paper.

Step 3

Clear the calculator. Give it and the paper back to your friend. Then ask her to:

• Multiply the last four digits of her phone number by 2.

• Add this answer to the last number written on the paper.

Step 4

• Subtract 250 from the sum now on the piece of paper.

• Divide the new number by 2.

The answer will be your friend's phone number!

Eww...

Said Mrs. Turkey to young Tom:

"If your father could see you now, he'd turn over in his gravy."

What's invisible and smells like a banana?

A monkey fart.

What's invisible and smells like a carrot?

A rabbit fart.

LITTLE GIRL: HOW MUCH ARE THOSE PUPPIES IN THE WINDOW?

PET STORE OWNER: TWENTY DOLLARS APIECE.

LITTLE GIRL: HOW MUCH IS A WHOLE ONE?

Why did the toilet paper roll down the hill?

It wanted to get to the bottom!

WHAT creatures DID NOT TO GO INTO NOAH'S ARK IN PAIRS? THE maggots. THEY WENT IN APPLES.

SCABS ON TOAST

What You Need

- Toaster
- Plate
- Butter knife
- Band-Aid

- 12 to 16 raisins
- 2 slices of bread
- Butter or margarine
- Your favorite jam

Preparation

1. Take the raisins and rip them into scab-size pieces.

2. Toast the bread and set it on the plate (don't burn your fingers!). Spread each slice with butter and jam.

3. Then place the "scabs" all over the bread—and eat!

The Prank

Now it's time to gross out a friend. Stick a raisin "scab" on the gauze part of a Band-Aid (don't let them see you do it!). Stick the Band-Aid on your arm or leg. Then tell your friend you're so hungry you could eat a scab. Watch them gag as you whip off the bandage and chow down.

"DOCTOR! DOCTOR! WHAT DID THE X-RAY OF MY HEAD SHOW?"

"NOTHING."

"Doctor! Doctor! I feel like I'm turning into a bear!"

"How long have you felt this way?"

"Ever since I was a cub."

"Doctor! Doctor! No one pays attention to me."

"Next!"

In the middle of a game, the coach pulled one of his young players aside and said, "Do you understand what cooperation is? Do you understand what a team is?"

The little boy nodded yes.

"Do you understand that what matters is whether we win together as a team?"

The little boy nodded again.

"So, when a strike is called or when you're out at first," the coach continued, "you don't argue or curse or attack the umpire. Do you understand all that?"

Again the little boy nodded.

"Good," said the coach. "Now go over there and explain it to your mother."

285

YOU NAME IT

SILLY PET NAMES

These are real pet names. How many silly pet names can you think up?

CATS
Tater Tot
Anchovy
Bouncer
Ali Kat
Catfish
Fishbone
Boomerang
Wrinkle

DOGS
Ninja
Shredder
Whizzer

CAT PAIRS
Ben & Jerry
Calvin & Hobbes
Simba & Nala
Monty & Python
Tigger & Eeyore
Sweet & Sour
Peeka & Boo

DOG PAIRS
Rif & Raf
Zig & Zag
Nickel & Dime
Pete & Repeat
Razzle & Dazzle
Ping & Pong
Nacho & Chip

CATS
Anestophles
(A-nest-o'fleas)

Mao Tse-tung
(Mousey Tongue)

DOGS
Nightmare
Puddles
Hobo
Knockout
Hoover
(eats anything)
Gizmo

Logic puzzles

MYSTERY MAN

The police have found the body of a man face down in the desert. He's wearing a backpack. There are no footprints around him. How did he die?

DOUBLE DEATH

Fred and Ethel are dead. Their bodies were found lying on the floor in a puddle of water. Broken glass lies scattered around them. Who were Fred and Ethel, and how did they die?

Give up? The solutions are on the next page.

Solutions

Answers for the previous page.

MYSTERY MAN

He jumped out of an airplane.
The backpack is his parachute,
which failed to open.

DOUBLE DEATH

Fred and Ethel are goldfish. The
aquarium was knocked over and
broke on the floor, spilling the
water and poor Fred and Ethel.

LIMERICKS

Here's another batch of
Uncle John's favorite
limericks.

There was a young
fellow named Weir,
Who hadn't an atom of fear.
He indulged a desire
To touch a live wire.
(Most any last line
will do here!)

I'd rather have fingers
than toes;
I'd rather have ears than a nose;
And as for my hair,
I'm glad it's all there;
I'll be awfully sad when it goes.

A Bird Joke

A man saw a beautiful parrot in a pet store with a blue string hanging from one foot and a red one from the other. He thought this was a bit odd so he asked the owner what the strings were for. "This is a highly trained parrot," the owner replied.

"If you pull the red string he talks in French, if you pull the blue string he talks in English."

"What happens if you pull them both at the same time?" the man asked.

"I fall off my perch, you idiot!" shouted the parrot.

A TRUE STORY

A group of students were sitting around talking about the awful things that had happened to them on Friday the 13th. When one of the kids mentioned that there was going to be a Friday the 13th the next month, a girl who had been silent during the conversation, suddenly announced, "Well, if Friday the 13th is on a Monday, I'm not coming to school!"

How do you get an
elephant to the top
of an oak tree?

Plant an acorn under
him and wait 50 years.

What if I don't want
to wait 50 years?

Put a parachute on the
elephant and drop him
from an 'elecopter.

How do you get an
elephant down from
an oak tree?

Tell him to sit on
a leaf and wait
until autumn.

Why are alligators
long and flat?

They must have
gotten too close
to the oak tree.

ELEPHANT Jokes

Why did the elephant wear dark sunglasses?

So he wouldn't be recognized.

What did Tarzan say when he saw the elephant coming up over the hill?

Nothing. He didn't recognize him.

Artsy-Fartsy

Three stinky limericks.

There once was a
man from Rangoon,
Whose farts could be heard
on the moon.
When you'd least expect 'em,
They'd burst from his rectum
With the force of a raging typhoon!

There once was a
girl from La Plata,
Who was often employed as a farta.
Her deafening reports
At the Argentine sports
Made her much in demand
as a starta.

There was a young
fellow from Sparta,
A really magnificent farta.
On the strength of one bean
He'd fart "God Save the Queen,"
And Beethoven's *Moonlight Sonata*.

More
WORD PUZZLES

*Got a minute? See if
you can make sense
of these wordplays.*

1. millio1n

2. land time

3. gegs

4. BB
   or
   ~~BB~~

5. _____et

6. ice³

7.
   it's it's

  its   it's

 it's   it's

  it's   it's

    it's it's

*Answers are on
the next page.*

MORE WORD PUZZLES

1. One in a million.
2. Land before time.
3. Scrambled eggs.
4. 2 be or not 2 be.
5. Blanket.
6. Ice cube.
7. It's going around.

HOW INSULTING!

Yo' mama's house is so small, she has to go outside to change her mind.

Yo' daddy is so old, when he was young, rainbows were black and white.

Yo' sister's breath smells so bad, that when she yawns her teeth duck.

Yo' brother is so dirty, he has to creep up on bathwater.

Yo' brother is so stupid, he took a spoon to the Super Bowl.

Yo' daddy is so old, he sat behind Jesus in the third grade.

Yo' mama is so fat, she can't even jump to a conclusion.

Yo' daddy is so old, when he was born the Dead Sea was just getting sick.

Yo' mama is so short, she can hang glide with Doritos.

FOR SALE:
Police dog. Will
eat anything.
Very fond of
children.

MORE EPITAPHS

Who says that death is no laughing matter? Certainly not the writers of these inscriptions found on real tombstones.

IN HARTSCOMBE, ENGLAND:

On the 22nd of June Jonathan Fiddle Went out of tune.

IN LONDON:

HERE LIES OWEN MOORE
GONE AWAY
OWIN' MORE
THAN HE COULD PAY.

In Richmond, Virginia:

She always said her feet were killing her...but nobody believed her.

GAMES

SILLY FUN

Bored? More suggestions from Uncle John, the Funmeister.

1. Deliver balloon messages. Write silly messages (happy thoughts, riddles, silly jokes) on balloons and hand them to random people.

2. Play water balloon air ball. Fill a water balloon with water and toss it into the air. The object of the game is to keep the balloon in the air, so once you catch it, you must immediately toss it to someone else. It's a good idea to have lots of water balloons already filled and ready to go. The fun really kicks in when the water balloons start breaking.

Phh-art

A woman went to see a doctor about a problem. She told him she was always ripping nasty farts that she could never smell or hear. The doctor thought about it, then gave her some pills and told her to come back next week.

"So how are we doing?" the doctor asked when she returned.

"Well, I'm still having these horrible farts," she said, "but now they smell like rotten eggs."

The doctor nodded. "Okay, now that we've cleared up your sinuses, let's get to work on your hearing..."

Does Your Name Equal Your Job?

A. J. and H. A. Barker wrote The Complete Book of Dogs.

Five Names for Pairs of Dogs

1. Thunder & Lightning
2. Rocky & Bullwinkle
3. Rough & Tumble
4. Biscuit & Gravy
5. Rif & Raf

ODDS...

Jokes, facts, and other left-overs.

REAL NAMES OF REAL PEOPLE

Adam Baum
Grace Moke
Denver Maier
Ima Bird

Swallows sit exactly six inches apart on a wire.

IN BRITISH COLUMBIA, IT IS ILLEGAL TO KILL A SASQUATCH.

What is a free gift? Aren't all gifts free?

You're not allowed to remove bandages in public in Canada.

If you go into the bathroom an American and come out American, what are you while you're in the bathroom?

European!

...'N' ENDS

FOUR NAMES FOR PAIRS OF CATS
1. PITTER & PATTER
2. JACK & JILL
3. SALT & PEPPER
4. NIP & TUCK

Four Real Doctors' Names:
1. Cynthia Rasch
2. James D. Cure
3. John Spine
4. Charles Paine Bonebrake

YOU'RE GROUNDED

A ROTTEN PRANK

Rubber Ducky

Know anyone who has a five-gallon water dispenser? Before installing the next water bottle, squeeze a small rubber ducky into it. Then turn the bottle upside down on the dispenser and wait!

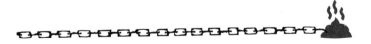

GROSS JOKES

Two cannibals were eating a clown, and one said, "Does this taste funny to you?"

What is the last thing to go through a bug's mind when he hits the windshield?

His butt!

What's grosser than gross?

Eating raisin bran when your brother can't find his scab collection!

Why did the umpire bring toilet paper to the game?

Because the bases were loaded!

WHO LIKES DISGUSTING THINGS MORE, A DOG OR THE SON OF A SUPERMARKET OWNER?

THE SON. HE'S A LITTLE GROCER!

Why was the sand wet?

Because the sea-weed!

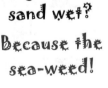

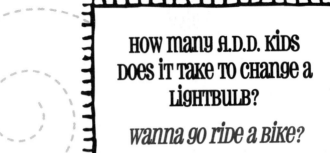

HOW MANY A.D.D. KIDS
DOES IT TAKE TO CHANGE A
LIGHTBULB?

wanna go ride a bike?

How many jugglers
does it take to change
a lightbulb?

*One—but it takes
at least three
light bulbs.*

How many Valley girls does it
take to change a lightbulb?

Oooh, like, manual labor?
Gag me with a spoon! As if!

A TRUE STORY

A burglar surprised an 87-year-old Delaware man in his house one Sunday morning. "Stay still," the robber told the old man, "and you won't get hurt."

"Okay," the old man replied, "but may I go to the bathroom?"

"Sure," the robber said.

The old man then climbed out of the bathroom window and called 9-1-1 from a neighbor's house.

MORE CHICKEN RIDDLES

Why did the duck cross the road?
*Because the chicken retired and
moved to Florida.*

Why did the otter cross the road?
To get to the otter side.

Why did the chicken cross the basketball court?
She heard the referee calling fowls.

Why did the wasp cross the road?
It had to go to the waspital.

Why did the rabbit cross the road?
To get to the hopping mall.

Why did the fish cross the river?
To get to its school.

Why did the chewing gum cross the road?
It was stuck to the chicken.

YOU NAME IT

MORE REAL PUNNY NAMES

Ever wish you had a different name? Imagine how you'd feel if you had one of these.

Hugo First

Ann Teaks

Dwight Stuff

Barb Dwyer

Hedda Hare

Eileen Dover

Brock O'Lee

Ivana B. Alone

Chester Drawers

Giovanni Frye-Swithdat

Dale E. Bread

Polly Warner-Cracker

Claire DeRoom

Hank R. Chief

Enzo D. Urth

Chick Pease

Ben Dover

C. U. Sunday

Denton Fender

Haley Scommett

Elmer Sklue

Dan DeLyon

Carmen Denominator

Jess U. Waite

Hammond Eggs

THE WORMS CRAWL IN

Don't ever laugh when a hearse rolls by,
For you may be the next to die.
They'll wrap you up in a dirty sheet
And put you down about 30 feet.
Things are fine for about a week,
And then the coffin begins to leak.
Little green bugs with big green eyes
Crawl in your nostrils and out your fly.
The worms crawl in, the worms crawl out,
The worms play Monopoly on your snout.
Your eyes turn red, your skin turns green,
Your pus comes out like whipping cream.
You sop it up with a piece of bread,
And that's what you eat when you are dead.

A LOGIC PUZZLE

STICK 'EM UP!

A man walks into a tavern and asks for a glass of water. Suddenly the bartender pulls a gun on him. The man says, "Thank you," and leaves.

What happened?

You'll find the answer on the next page.

Solution

STICK
'EM UP!

Answer for the previous page.

The man had the hiccups.
The bartender pulled the
gun to frighten the man...
which made his hiccups
go away.

HAPPY / SAD
GEORGE

Now you see him smile, now you don't. Try this origami using George Washington's face on a one dollar bill. Then try it with Abe Lincoln on a five.

Step 1: Make two vertical mountain folds that intersect the pupils of George's eyes.

Step 2: Now put a vertical valley fold exactly between the eyes.

Step 3: Tilt the dollar away from you and George smiles.

Step 4: Tilt the bill toward you and George frowns.

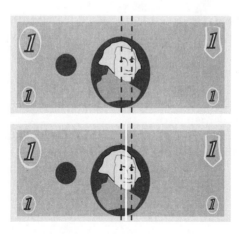

YOU NAME IT

YOUR NAME = YOUR JOB?

*Will your name foretell your job? It certainly
did for these people. (Better hope your
name isn't Seymour Butts!)*

Ashley Burns is a fire fighter.

John Looney is a psychiatrist.

A. M. Glass wrote *Optical Materials*.

M. Bedrock is a geologist.

Tom DeLay and **John Doolittle** are politicians.

Robert Cropp is an agricultural inspector.

Dr. Moneypenny lectures on banking.

David Butcher works for the Society for the Prevention of Cruelty to Animals.

David Steele wrote *The Chemistry of Metallic Elements*.

Barry Mason is a stone sculptor.

Alan Pee cleans cesspools.

Michael Lean teaches nutrition.

Michael Achey is a doctor.

David Killingray wrote *The Atom Bomb*.

KNOCK KNOCK JOKES

Knock-knock!
Who's there?
Europe.
Europe who?
Yer a poo, too.

Knock-knock!
Who's there?
Euripides.
Euripides who?
Euripides pants,
I breaka
your
face.

YOUR TURN!

Here's your big chance to let us know what you want in the next edition of Uncle John's Bathroom Reader for Kids Only. *Write it down here, cut it out, and send it to us.*

_____

_____

_____

_____

_____

_____

_____

_____

_____

_____

Uncle John's Bathroom Reader
For Kids Only!

Uncle John's Bathroom Reader
For Kids Only!
Copyright © 2002. $12.95
288 pages, illustrated.

Uncle John's **Electrifying**
Bathroom Reader For Kids Only!
Copyright © 2003. $12.95
288 pages, illustrated.

Uncle John's **Top Secret!**
Bathroom Reader For Kids Only!
Copyright © 2004. $12.95
288 pages, illustrated.

To order, contact:
Bathroom Readers' Press
P.O. Box 1117, Ashland, OR 97520
Phone: 888-488-4642 Fax: 541-482-6159
www.bathroomreader.com

THE LAST PAGE

FELLOW BATHROOM READERS:
Bathroom reading should never be taken loosely—we must sit firmly for what we believe in, even while the rest of the world is taking pot shots at us.

So Sit Down and Be Counted! Join the Bathroom Readers' Institute. It's free! Send a self-addressed, stamped envelope and your email address to: Bathroom Readers' Institute, P.O. Box 1117, Ashland, Oregon 97520. You'll receive a free membership card, our BRI newsletter (sent out via e-mail), discounts when ordering directly through the BRI, and you'll earn a permanent spot on the BRI honor roll!

UNCLE JOHN'S NEXT
BATHROOM READER FOR KIDS ONLY
IS ALREADY IN THE WORKS!

Is there a subject you'd like to read about in our next *Uncle John's Bathroom Reader For Kids Only?* Write to us or contact us through our website and let us know. We aim to please.

Well, we're out of space, and when you've got to go, you've got to go. Hope to hear from you soon. Meanwhile, remember:

Go with the Flow!